I0022264

White Folks Guide to Understanding the Black Community and Get Out the Vote

by

Pastor Shannon Wright

Pastor Shannon Wright

Copyright © 2012 Nouveau Ink

ISBN 978-0615684277

Published in the United States by Nouveau Ink Publishers, Plainfield, New Jersey.

Printed in the United States of America on acid-free paper.

2012 First Edition

Nouveauinkpublishers.com

This book is dedicated to my husband Michael who is himself a wonderfully talented published author, who gave me the time and encouragement to do this, my children who need to know this, my sister Rhandi, and to my mother, Janeice, who I wish had lived long enough to see the book finished.

Love you all!

Pastor Shannon Wright

White Folks Guide to Understanding the Black Community

Table of Contents

Pastor Shannon Wright

Acknowledgements

I would like to thank the Nouveau team as a whole for another literary work of art. Brendan Sloan thank, you for all your hard work on all the graphics. To Aleksandra Stepniewski thank you for a wonderful job of editing this book. You are awesome. To Andrew Dinkel thank you for all your technical support and work on the websites. Thank you to Mr. William Dickerson for your insights on healthcare reform. Lastly thank you to Kuuleme Stephens for the inspiration from your Blog "The Last Civil Right". You tell it like it is and I look forward to working with you on many more projects.

Pastor Shannon Wright

Forward

Pastor Shannon Wright

For some reason the forward which is found in the beginning of the book is usually written at the end of the book. I say that because most authors start with why they have written the book. I am writing this at the beginning of my journey to explain why I am writing this chronicle.

I am a Black woman. I was born in America to a single teen Mother. My mother at the time was still living with her parents in the projects. This story may sound like countless of other stories, except for one thing. My Mother understood the value of education. She knew she wanted a different type of life than the one she saw her parents have. At an early age, she learned that education was the key.

My Mom taught me to believe that I could be and I could do anything I set my mind to. Because of her I decided to be active in my community and learn how and why society functions the way it does. While working in the community I met my husband.

Together my Mother and my husband encouraged me, supported me, consoled me, and sent me back out again into the world. They would not let me quit. Because of them I had the courage to compete and win several beauty pageants which gave me confidence. With conviction of the spirit instilled in me as a child courage and with my new found confidence, I have decided it's time to step up my game.

I owe it to not only my Mother's memory, but my husband, my children and my community.

If nothing else this book will make you think. It is my intention to inspire and to motivate everyone who reads this book to do something to benefit a community or segment of a community that they would not think of as their own. Only by coming out of our comfort zones can we understand or at least begin to understand those who are different than us and begin to try to walk even a half a mile in their shoes.

Kuuleme Stephens

My name is Kuuleme Stephens. I was born and raised in Tucson, Arizona. I was raised by my Great Grandmother and Great Grandfather. My mother and father were both heroin addicts. I barely knew my father, and my mother died when I was around two years of age of a heroin overdose. I grew up in an area of Tucson, called "Sugar Hill." It got its nickname due to the drugs that were being sold in the neighborhood and at the nearby park.

White Folks Guide to Understanding the Black Community

Growing up I attended mostly all white schools. Although we lived in the Tucson High School District (which was considered the bad school district at the time), my Great Grandmother chose to send my sister and me to the Amphitheater School District (which line started just a few streets over) using my Grandmother's address. I then went on to college and attended the University of Arizona for one year and then enlisted in the United States Navy as a Navy Hospital Corpsman. After getting medically discharged from the Navy, I returned to Tucson and attended Pima Community College where I earned my Certification for Emergency Medicine. I worked various jobs in the medical field, then went back to school at American InterContinental University for Business Administration and Criminal Justice. Since then I have worked at the Disabled American Veterans as an adjunct and I am currently a member of the DAV Honor Guard.

I am one of nine co-authors of The Last Civil Right (http://www.thelastcivilright.org/), and have functioned as a political consultant for some. I have appeared as a guest on numerous radio stations to talk about my political views as well. People often ask me what my political opinions are or some just assume. Well, I can tell you what I am.

I describe myself as a Black Female Independent Conservative. The Black and Female is easy to sell and understand, but most do not understand the meaning of the words Independent or Conservative. I consider myself an Independent because I do not care for Career politicians.

When I say career politicians I mean anyone (Democrat or Republican) who serves in a political position longer than 1 term. Also, one who has "grown up" in politics whose way has been paved for them, and they basically have been groomed to be a politician. In my opinion, "Career Politicians" are ruining our country, care only about themselves, and don't know anything about being and average American living in the United States.

When I see the word "Conservative" in describing myself, most people assume that I am a Republican. That simply is not true. My morals, thoughts, ideas, and viewpoints are considered to be along the conservative lines. I do not consider myself to be a Republican because I do differ in opinion on some things that are considered to be hard line issues for the Republican Party. I actually was "born" Democrat, later changed to being a Republican, and then switched to being Independent as I got older and more political savvy. I am also a mother of 3 (1 daughter and 2 nieces that I have guardianship of), a stepmother of 5 and a grandmother of 8.

I chose to be a contributing author for this book as an effort to answer questions that I get from people who want to know how to better relations with the Black Community in the political realm and in everyday life as well. I hope that my writing this will help in the efforts in understanding the Black Community!

In writing this book we do not claim to have invented or re-invented the wheel, we simply made it run better

Introduction

In order to understand the Black Community we must travel back in time. Slavery is a big part of the Black's History in America and it must be addressed and acknowledged appropriately. There is no way around addressing this sensitive issue as it is the very beginnings of Blacks in America.

In the beginning, Blacks were brought to America as slaves and against their will. They lost their homes, families, identities, culture and freedom. They were hunted down like animals by other Africans and Arabs who sold them to Slave Traders, and Whites. There began the hatred of whites for the Black Community.

When the Blacks were brought over as slaves, they didn't know the English language. Not knowing how to speak and understand the language nor how to read and write, plays a big part in the thinking and mindset of American Blacks today. The hatred of the white community was essentially created, bred, and past down generation after generation from that point forward. As everyone knows, hatred is a hard-thing to overcome. For example, if you hate the taste of fish, you usually tend to stay away from fish or anything that contains fish in it, right??? Well the same concept can be applied to people.

When the Civil War took place in 1861-1865, race was put on the forefront. Some would take the argument that race and the battle over slavery itself was not the main issue of the Civil War, but taxes and way of life were the issue. Regardless of the two, Blacks will always view the Civil War as a fight over slavery. Why??? Because this was the fight that made the difference between being a slave and a free person for them. In order for you to understand the Black Community, you must acknowledge and accept that as fact. The Civil war did indeed being change for the Black Community. With slavery banned, it ushered in a new era for Blacks. They were free, but.... free did not mean better off. As slaves were not allowed the freedoms of learning to read and write, most did not have the necessary tools to be independent. A lot of slaves stayed on the plantations as share croppers working for next to nothing, others ventured out on their own looking for a better life. Even as one's ventured off the plantations, they found that life hadn't much changed for them. Most whites still viewed Blacks as being beneath them and still treated them as such.

With little or no education, Blacks were limited in types of work that they could do. Jobs such as manual labor, maids, janitors, cooks, nannies, all things that white folks didn't want to do themselves, were really the only jobs that Black folks qualified for and could obtain. With the use of Blacks independence as a free people, so also came the rise of the hate groups, such as the Ku Klux Klan. Blacks being lynched, beaten, raped, and much more only because they were black, only fueled the fire for hatred and divide between the Black and White Communities.

White Folks Guide to Understanding the Black Community

You must be able to visualize yourself in their shoes, if you want to understand their thinking. Having physical and mental harm done to you is a powerful thing. Both leave an unimaginable amount of scars. Some people learn from these scars and try to improve things, and some people never get over them.

The ushering in of Separate but Equal made a big difference in the Black Community, it gave a sense of progress, but the Black Community was still not equal to whites overall. For example, Black restrooms were generally smaller, hardly working, filthy, not well lit, etc... Whereas white bathrooms were always kept up and had all amenities that were available at the time. The schools were not equal as well. Often there weren't enough school books or supplies, teachers often taught multiple grades due to lack of teachers in the Black Community and white teachers willing to teach in a Black School, and when there were text books available, they would often be used and out-dated.

During the Separate but Equal" age, Blacks were often forced to use the back door, forced to let whites ahead of them in lines, and not allowed to sit at public counters. Nothing was equal during this time period. The name ""Separate but Equal" was more like "Give Them Something so They'll Shut Up". Moving forward to present time, we are now in the age of "Equal Rights with Special Privileges". I use this term because now Blacks and other minorities know that all you have to do is get what you want is yell racism or discrimination. It has become the platform by which all minorities use to extort the system and remain dependant on others. So far this tactic is working well, but now with Conservatives becoming more drained, fed up, and more vocal; it is very apparent that eventually you do run out of other peoples' money and sympathy....

Part I

You can't judge a man 'till you walk a mile in his shoes, or better yet don't judge at all.

Who we are...

Chapter 1

Color is not just skin deep, it cuts to the bone

As a "light skinned" or "Virginia Redbone" female I learned at an early age it ain't just White folks that get stuck on color. My Black Brothers and sisters are just as color conscious.

FACT: From the days of slavery the light skinned Blacks got the "good" jobs. We were the "house niggas". We had it easier. Some of us in the big house were even taught to read so we could read to Master's children when the Misses was too busy.

Color is an issue even to this day. You hear Black folks even saying he or she is too light or dark. To understand us you must understand we are divided even amongst ourselves by color. The stigma of color from slavery days is still alive and well to this day.

It is widely believed in the Black community that light skinned Blacks get more breaks in life. Drive through the projects or go to a Welfare office and take notice of the Black women there. What percentage of them is light skinned, and what percentage of them is darker skinned? Conversely go to some of your better Universities and try the same thing. What do you think you will find?

This is a buy product of something called the slave mentality. For those of you who don't know what that means please allow me to explain. The slave mentality is the belief that someone needs to save you. In the words of Kuuleme T. Stephens who appeared on CBS Radio with Dan Rea and KLZ The Source with Kenneth Clark, a slave mentality is one of feeling inferior or feeling lost without hope. It is a feeling that we do not have the power to significantly alter our own circumstances. [1]

The following is an anonymous quote I found online as an individual definition or interpretation of slave mentality.

1. I have a word that I collate with "slave mentality" and that is "complacency". I think this is an affliction when people don't strive for anything better in their lives, maybe because they just accept what life hands them instead of taking charge of their future. You see this mentality mostly in urban slums; the people may feel trapped because they may not see a way out of that type of life condition. Everything and everyone

around them is negative, that's all they see, so that's all they know. It's a viscous cycle. I think many slaves had a similar attitude, and that's how the masters were able to keep them in their control for so long. [2]

*   *   *

More of us are born being taught our concrete, not glass ceiling is so low we need to be careful not to hit our heads, not to reach for the stars. Many of us are taught, "You Black, you always gonna be Black and ain't gonna get nowhere." There is a direct correlation between which philosophy you were taught and where you end up in your life.

The truth is that in this society the darker you are the harder you have to work to get to the same place as someone else of a fairer skin. Certainly it is a lot harder for a Black person than a White person to get to the same place. Whether this is true or not is a matter of opinion. However, that surely is what I teach mine!

You might ask me why? I want mine to know that they can be whatever they want if they are willing to work hard to get it. I want mine to know who and

21

what they are, and where they come from. I want mine to KNOW that the only limitations they are subject to are those they put on themselves. But I say again that we are not all taught this, and there is a direct correlation between philosophies and life choices.

I can tell you this, I have certainly heard in my life "You don't know what it is like to be really Black". The assumption being that because I am of a lighter complexion I have not had the same struggles as some of my darker brothers and sisters is simply not true.

I don't need to tell you that just as many Blacks are color struck as are many non- Blacks. The difference though is that in the Black community the belief is that non-Blacks either judge us by our skin-tone or paint us all with the same brush saying, "Black is Black and yall all Black." Again whether it is true or not is a matter of opinion. However, what is true is that you would be hard pressed not to find a Black person who did not have a story related to color.

As Martin Luther King said in his famous "I Have a Dream" speech: *"I have a dream that my four little children will one day live in a nation where they will not be judged by the color of their skin, but by the content of their character."*
– Martin Luther King, I Have a Dream Speech [3]

White Folks Guide to Understanding the Black Community

I too share that dream.

*   *   *

Just like Martin Luther King, I too have a dream. In my dreams I no longer feel compelled to remind my beautiful dark chocolate son that he is judged by a different set of standards. He no longer needs to hear me say that he must strive for excellence with the knowledge that his excellence will be dulled exponentially by the 50 shades of Black that is our skin.

In my dreams gone are the days of racial profiling. I no longer feel compelled to remind my beautiful Black children to be mindful of their clothes, behavior, location, and vernacular they use merely because not to be mindful could become a cause for "justifiable" homicide based on the color of their skin.

In my dreams gone are the days where the divides between us are as deep as the highest mountains are tall.

In my dreams, I am my brother's keeper to all my brothers and sisters regardless of race, creed, or color.

Because in my dream we have overcome; our Lord has seen us through. We have the victory and we are not afraid.

In my dreams the statement, "We the People" stands for all shades, hues, and pigments. We are working together in order to form a more perfect union. Justice is color blind to ensure domestic tranquility and to provide for a common defense. We promote the general Welfare of all, and we secure the Blessings of Liberty to ourselves and our Posterity Irregardless of our skin because that I say to you is the true spirit this great nation was founded on.

We are a people of many hues, pigments, and shades. We range from alabaster to ebony. We are beautiful in our own right. We live, laugh, and we love. At our core we are all motivated by the same factors. If you must judge, judge us by the content of our character or not at all.

Chapter 2

Don't Judge a Book by Its Cover

In this country there are many types of profiling, and racial profiling is but one of many. If you are a blue-eyed blonde you may not be so bright, if you are Asian you must be smart, and so on. Let's be really clear on this, however, racial profiling is probably the only type of profiling that can get you killed.

One morning my oldest son, who at the time was majoring in electrical engineering, was on his way to school. It was the tail end of the morning rush hour, and he had just gotten off the train and was walking a few blocks to catch the bus to get to campus. He had on a jacket, jeans with a belt, and sneakers. He was carrying a messenger bag with his books in it and his laptop. As I said previously his pants were belted, his shoes tied, and he was not wearing a hat. As he walked down the street a police car drove beside him. He was told to stop by the police officers. The officers questioned him, asking why he was there, and where he was going. They also asked him for his I.D and ran it. When they were done my son asked them a valid question. He asked the officers why they had stopped him. The officers responded that they were just doing their job. Their answer was not that they got a call or that there was an incident, and he fit the description, it was just, "We are doing our job."

If it had been me, having a few more years of experience than my son, I would have asked as sweetly as pie—what exactly was that job that they were doing? I would have addressed the officer by name and shield number. I would have then explained that as a tax paying citizen, I was merely doing my own job of making sure that my tax dollars, and my neighbors' tax dollars were being well spent on police officers that were properly policing our communities.

Now, had it been me, being female and light skinned, this probably would not have happened. When my son told me what had happened to him, I was very upset and concerned .He told me that he was OK and that it was not a big deal. He said, "Mom, it happens a lot. It's part of being Black." At that moment, I was torn between a mix of powerful emotions. I was proud of my son and angry at the situation. First of all, I was immensely proud of my son that he could recognize what that was all about. I was proud of him that he did not allow the humiliation and embarrassment of being stopped on the street like a criminal, to make him react in the ignorant and emotional way we are perceived to act. But, I was also, incredibly saddened that still today in this great nation my 19 year old, well mannered, intelligent, and well-spoken, son could still be penalized for, as we call it, "walking while Black".

*　　　　　*　　　　　*

Unless you have been stopped, questioned, or persecuted for something as basic as the color of your skin, you have no idea how devastating it can be. Such an experience can drastically affect your psychological well-being. You don't know what it is like to walk down the street and know that for no other reason, but the color of your skin, you can be targeted, disliked, wrongly accused, and even persecuted. We may not be the only group of people in this country that can claim this; but, when you combine that with being brought here against our will, and then being enslaved, we are the only people to endure that trifecta and it's after effects.

According to The New Dictionary of Cultural Literacy, the English idiom "don't judge a book by its cover"[4] is a metaphorical phrase which means "you shouldn't prejudge the worth or value of something, by its outward appearance alone."

The Bible says: "Judge not lest yea be judged [5] and let yea without sin cast the first stone [6]." Let's break that down for a minute. 'Judge not lest yea be judged", means that unless you want to be judged, you don't judge others. "Let yea without sin cast the first stone", means that, since all have sinned and have fallen short of glory, there are none amongst us without sin. Therefore, no one on God's green Earth is qualified to judge anyone.

You know how every school has at least one of those kids that just doesn't fit. I mean their family lived in your town for generations, and you've known them since you were little. Maybe, you don't even know why they don't fit. You know the one that everybody picks on, ignores, or looks at funny? No matter how hard that person tries, they just don't fit in. Now, imagine that was you. For some of you reading this book, it was you. It may have been something as simple as your hair, the clothes you wore, the way you talked differently, or "they" just didn't like you. As time passed, everyone grew up and became adults, and it didn't matter anymore. Now, imagine even when you have grown up, people still think you don't fit in. Now, imagine it is based on the one thing in this world you can't change, the color of your skin. We call that bullying, and it is a punishable criminal offense.

White Folks Guide to Understanding the Black Community

*The Wikipedia definition of bullying is: form
of aggressive behavior manifested by the use of force or
coercion to affect others, particularly when the behavior
is habitual and involves an imbalance of power. It can
include verbal harassment,
physical assault or coercion and may be directed
repeatedly towards particular victims, perhaps on
grounds of race, religion, gender, sexuality, or
ability. The "imbalance of power" may be social power
and/or physical power. The victim of bullying is
sometimes referred to as a "target".* [6]

Many states have passed anti-bullying laws. The laws pertain to intimidation, harassment, and physical acts. Some of the things according to these laws, that are considered bullying, are wearing gang paraphernalia or other clothing to intimidate or exclude; Spreading rumors or posting degrading, harmful, or explicit pictures or messages or information using social media;. Taunting or making sexual slurs based on gender or sexual status; Name –calling, joking, or offensive remarks about a person's religion gender ethnicity or socio-economic status; and of course the physical abuse. The penalty's for such behavior can include civil fines and criminal penalties like, yes jail time depending on the specifics of the incident.

This brings me to an interesting point. When you judge someone according to their skin color, and act as if you have the right to treat that person any way you want, you could be the one ending up with the criminal record, instead of the one you thought had a record, as you assumed, based on the color of their skin.

So consider this. The next time you are walking down the street, and it is in the middle of the day in an average "safe" neighborhood, and you see a Black person approaching, and by approaching I mean walking down the street heading in the direction you came from, instead of crossing the street or clutching your wallet or purse, just smile. I guarantee a couple of things will happen. The first is you might get a smile back. More importantly, you may make someone's day that really needed it.

Chapter 3

Give a man a fish, you feed him for a day, but teach him to fish, and you feed him for life.[7]

Stop giving away the fish!!!!!! If I know that when I get hungry, I can come to you and get a fish, and I don't have to go fishing, then I am going to come to you, especially if I don't know how to fish. Now, let's look at this in another way. If you teach me how to fish, I can fish with you. I can help you reach and "feed" more people. At the very least, I can fish for my own family, which will in turn lighten your burden.

Entitlement programs that enable do more harm than good. From what I have studied, the bulk of the entitlement programs we have today are part of or stem from the seeds planted from President Franklin Delano Roosevelt's New Deal, which was his answer to the Great Depression of the 1930's.

There are a few things of importance about President Franklin Delano Roosevelt and the New Deal.

1. Many of the programs were and are the predecessors of the programs that are alive and well today.
2. These programs were part of FDR's platform to win the presidency.
3. For FDR to win, he needed the votes of the poor and the Black.

This was a turning point in our history. It was the first time when a conscious decision was made to buy the presidency through programs that were never meant to last. These programs were meant to be a quick fix to win the election. These programs, many of which in some shape or form, are still around today were the beginning of pacifying and dumbing- down of the Black population.

Although we had had the right to vote for some time now, this was one of the first campaigns that courted our vote. Under FDR's New Deal people, who just 3 generations ago were slaves, were now being given things by the same government that enslaved them. We supported this; we embraced this at surface value because we were being recognized. This campaign orchestrated the shift in the political alignment of Blacks. This made the Democratic Party the party of the people.

White Folks Guide to Understanding the Black Community

Most of you reading this may already know. But, most Blacks don't. If you asked most Black people if they knew that there was a point in time when many Black people were Republican, they would say you were lying. They would not believe you.

Until recently, I was a Democrat. My parents and Grand Parents were Democrats. In my family, you are Black, and you are a Democrat. It wasn't until I began to home school my children that this issue came up out of the mouths of babes. We were doing a history lesson on Fredrick Douglas and his politics.

We talked about the fact that Fredrick Douglas was Synonymous with the word conservative. Frederick Douglass' Republicans are people who champion the LIFE-EMPOWERING values of Douglass. They are: (1) Respect for the Constitution, (2) Respect for Life, (3) Belief in Limited Government, and (4) Belief in Personal Responsibility. A "black dyed in the wool Republican" that was the quintessential conservative Republican. He was a catalyst in the Abolitionist Movement that gave birth to the Republican Party and ended slavery. His political views lined up with the beliefs of the Founding Fathers. [8]

At the end of the lesson, my son said, "Well, you sound like him, so why are you a Democrat?" I didn't have a good answer for him. I told him, "Because, when I first registered to vote, I didn't know all the things you know", and we both laughed.

The truth is that in my family you were a democrat, period. We were taught the Democrats were the ones trying to help us. They recognized the error of their fore-fathers ways and wanted to make amends. That's what we were taught. As for the Republicans, they were just a bunch of rich White folks who didn't give a rat's butt about Black folks.

It was not until writing this that my true enlightenment began. You see as a people it has not been that many generations since we were slaves. My grandparents, on my Mother's side of the family, were children of the first generation of freemen. My great-grandparents were sharecroppers in the South. They didn't read. They knew what they were told. Both my grandfather and grandmother, on my mother's side, moved north with their parents when they were young. They could read and had some "schooling". My grandfather was former military and then worked in construction; my grandmother worked in hospitals.

Even though we had the right to vote since 1870, because of the 15th amendment voting for was not always easy or safe to do. When my mother was born in the 40's, my grandparents were reaping some of the benefits' of FDR's New Deal. They had some services, rights, and benefits that they never had. They were grateful. We owed that gratitude to the Democrats for helping us Black folks. My grandparents didn't look the gift horse in the mouth.

I was born in the late 60's, which was after the Civil Rights Act. The Civil Rights Act was another gift from the Democrats that further secured the fact that Black meant Democrat. My story is but one of millions. It's only been 3 generations, maybe 4, since our ancestors were freed. For some of you, it took 3 or 4 generations to get your heads on straight, and you all came here by choice, under your own free will.

*   *   *

If you ask most Black people if anyone in their family has ever been on welfare, the answer would most likely be a big, "Yes". But understand there are 2 different categories. One category is those that accepted public assistance, and used it only when needed and in the manner in which it was intended. In the other category, are those that use the system as if it were their birth right. They get every benefit from every program they can, and they milk it for everything they can. They act as if not only are they entitled, but you are obligated to enable them to do nothing, and let them sit back and collect, while taxpayers pay the bill.

Have you ever wondered what makes the difference between these two categories, between these two types of people? The ones that are striving for more, and are not complacent, have a strong sense of family values. They believe they can do better. They have their self respect, and their family pride to strive to do better. The "assistance" that they receive is a temporary bump in the road. But, category 2 is different. In this category, these folks have a multi-generational view of entitlement. What that means is that mom and grandma are both on public assistance, and they have instilled nothing better in their children. Most likely they come from a broken, one parent, household with much less parenting than they should have had.

Here's the part you may not be aware of, but I hope you can understand. You can't expect people to teach things to their children that they themselves were not taught without intervention. If you have a 30 year old grandmother, I guarantee you, there was an issue in her home, and that behavior is what then is passed down inadvertently, as it may be, to the next generation.

The problems we see in today's society are made exponentially worse by the erosion and breakdown of the family, in general and specifically in the African American community. There are different schools of thought as to how and when this started. If you believe the Moynihan Report [8], from the 1960's, there is more the government can and should do, but the bulk of the responsibility rests on the individual. The other side of that argument screamed "Foul!" and says, "You can't blame the victim".

Regardless to which school of thought you subscribe to, the numbers speak the truth. Since the 1960's, the amount of children being born out of wedlock is up, the amount of people getting married is down, and for those that do get married, divorce is still up. The number of single parent households is up. The traditional family has become an endangered species. You know the family where mom and dad are both in the home with the children? Where the children see dad or mom and dad works and comes home and teaches them wrong from right? That family is disappearing fast.

My husband, Michael, grew up without his father. His parents divorced when he was young. He would joke around that he learned how to be a man from watching television. Now, that is kind of scary, and a sad thought, considering a lot of what is on television now is not so great. He was fortunate that his mother had a very strong sense of values, especially her commitment to the family. When she wasn't working her 2 jobs, she spent as much time as she could with her children. The fact that she had 2 jobs; she really didn't have much time. The "role models" that Michael found on the streets of his South Bronx neighborhood were scarcely what any parent would or should want for their own children. He would watch the Cosby Show from time to time, but never even imagined that any Black folks could actually live like that. By the grace of God, his Mother was strong and taught him right from wrong. He was one of the fortunate ones. He knew there was something more and better out there; he strived to find it.

If the family is truly the cornerstone of the community, and the statistics are accurate, we are all in trouble. Am I my brother's keeper? Yes, I am [9]. It's time we learn how to keep all our brothers as individual citizens without a legislative mandate.

Chapter 4

To be a good teacher you must first be a good listener.

Most schools today have classes for English language learners. When you hire a teacher for the class what do you look for? I would think you would want someone who is compassionate towards people, passionate about education, and someone who is dedicated, right? What about being multi lingual? How well do you think it would work if the person you hire to teach a class for English language learners does not speak the native language of the students? It would be very difficult. The same principle applies here. You can't teach me if you can't understand me or communicate with me.

"If you want to hide something from a black person, hide it in a book"

That "joke" is one most Blacks and a lot of non – Blacks have heard. It doesn't mean we don't know how to read it means we don't like to read. Well that's the stereotype anyway.

FACT: During slavery time it was illegal for Blacks to be taught to read and write. The most oppressive limits on slave education were a reaction to Nat Turner's Revolt, in Southampton County, Virginia, during the summer of 1831. The ignorance of the slaves was considered necessary to the security of the slaveholders. Not only did owners fear the spread of specifically abolitionist materials, they did not want slaves to question their lot; thus, reading and reflection were to be prevented at any cost. The same legislation required that any black preacher needed to be given permission to speak before appearing at any congregation. [10]

White Folks Guide to Understanding the Black Community

Most people who have a heart for community work see a need and put together a plan, and then they set out to put the plan into action. However, a very important step, that is so often overlooked, is that those who you intend to "save" may not want your help. This is especially true if you give the impression that whatever it is you are doing is from a misguided place. You will be met with suspicion and mistrust which will simply undermine your efforts and eventually feel you are wasting your time.

To teach the Black community you must first understand the Black community. I don't mean the stereotypes of us liking fried chicken, watermelon, and greens, amongst other things, but to really try to understand our communities.

*   *   *

In doing my research for this section, I wanted to see if I could find anything written on the subject of teaching Black children. I included the essay I found in the apendix of this book for several reasons. When I started reading it I almost closed it. I was horrified and embarrassed that someone would feel so strongly about and negatively about teaching Black children. I thought of the children I had raised. I say it that way because I wanted to think of them as individuals, independent of me.

Let me remind you all at this point again, I was born to a single teen mom living in the projects. But let me clearly state, the kind of behavior described in this essay was in no way tolerated by my parents; and, such behavior was in no way tolerated by my husband or me at home. All that being said, schools like the one described here are all over the country. Some right here in my own town, and that was partly the reason we made the choice to home-school our children.

It saddens me greatly to hear educators speak as if they believe Black children are a waste. It saddens many others as well. It makes you feel as if instead of correcting the problem you have to defend the children almost enabling the disruptive and often unacceptable behavior.

The "system" has been in disarray for so long, that many have come to accept it as the norm; they have, lowered the standards we know to be right, in order to meet the reality of how things are in our communities. This cannot continue.

This section was supposed to be about listening to and understanding Black children in order to properly teach them. But to convey the significance of this, you would first need to understand what thoughts our children have, what is on their minds, and in their hearts, as they go to school. Many Black children are from single parent homes. Since it is a proven fact that statistically Blacks earn less than Whites for the same work, if a Black child comes from a single parent household, they most likely come from a financially disadvantaged family. The parent that is in the home is either dysfunctional or a loving functioning parent (who is working hard and long to make ends meet). However, in either scenario, it usually means that child may not be properly supervised.

If the household is dysfunctional, then clearly that child is going to be lacking in some areas through no fault of their own. When multi- generational dysfunctions are present, meaning parents unable to supervise the next generation of parents, well it's not surprising that a parent cannot teach their child something they have not been taught. For a well meaning single parent household, for instance, there is usually no time or energy for things like decorum to be taught in the home, as the author of the essay mentions. (See appendix)

When a parent sends their child to school, it is not to be judged, it's to be educated. The first step to being able to educate a Black child is to understand and listen to our Black children. If you can't hear them and they can't hear you metaphorically speaking, they are not getting educated. Even in a zoo you don't train someone for snakes and send them in to take care of the birds. Why should our children accept any less?

Part II

What We Want

At our core we all want the same things for ourselves and our families

Chapter 5

School is More than Books, Bricks, and Mortar

A school should be more than just bricks and mortar. A school should be a safe haven. A school should be an incubator for thoughts, ideas, and philosophies. Schools should have a mix of educators, parents, faith and community leaders, and other important people, coming together to mold and shape, and empower our future generations.

As you may have noticed, I didn't mention academics. Today, unfortunately when it comes down to school systems, the first priority for parents is worrying about whether their child is even safe in school. Too many of our urban schools have become breading grounds for criminal activity. We want our children to be safe.

I have known for some time now that safety has been an issue in our urban and even suburban schools. This was a deciding factor when it came down to the decision of home schooling my children. For most of us there is a moment when enough is enough; when you know that it is time to change. There is a moment, when your new life mission is to fix something you see as so wrong, that you just can't feel good about anything, until you try to fix it. For me, that moment came in September of 2009.

I got a call from a grandmother who was distraught. On the second day of school, her grandson had been approached by some students in school. There was an argument. It wasn't a major dispute because her grandson decided, "not to go there" with them as we like to say. He kept it from escalating at the time and continued his day.

At the end of the school day, as he and his friends were leaving school, someone approached him and attempted to start a fight on behalf of the young man who had started the fight earlier. The situation escalated. One thing lead to another and the young man was shot.

I went with the grandmother to the hospital to see the young man for a prayer meeting and to just speak to the young man. He confirmed what I suspected. The incident was gang related. The young man, who was shot, was not a gang member, but the other young men were. Now, I know there are 3 sides to every story; one side, the other side, and somewhere in the middle, there is the truth of it all. I also know that there may have been some details the young man had omitted because his grandmother was there.

The most disturbing part of this whole story was that when the grandmother and I went to the school to speak with the principal, we were told that there wasn't one. We were told that, although the school was indeed open, the new principal was not due to start, until the following week. Now, let me ask, how many of you would find that acceptable? Not many, I'm sure. Unfortunately, this is the kind of thing that regularly goes on in our minority communities. We want our children to be safe in school, and preferably, safe and educated.

Chapter 6

Jobs We Can Feel Good About

To write this chapter, I spoke with people that were working and people that were unemployed. I asked them a simple question, what do they want? The answers fell into a couple of different categories, but the main theme was the same. Everyone wanted jobs they could feel good about.

I don't want to talk about the minority of minorities. They are employed albeit in significantly lower numbers than their White counterparts in white collar jobs. This isn't about the Black doctors, lawyers, or engineers. This isn't about the Black teachers, accountants, or even civil servants. This is about the cashiers, greeters, and the unemployed.

I spoke with one gentleman, who is a father and a husband. He grew up in a single parent household. He was raised by a single mother who worked two jobs. His mother had instilled in him the importance of working. Because of that, he got his first job when he was sixteen, and he worked consistently after that. He left school to work full time to help his family. He met a young lady and started a family of his own. When his children were still young, he went back to school and got his G.E.D..

With his G.E.D., he got a better job. Then, a few years later, the company he worked for lost their largest contract and he lost his job. When he attempted to find a new job, he was asked if he had a degree. He did not.

His mother had instilled the importance of working and being accountable for himself and his family. She did not however stress the importance of education beyond high school. She had never made it to high school. No one in his family had attended college.

He is now a part of the rest of the 40 something percentage of people that cannot find jobs to take care of their families. He has been trying, but to no avail. His children are old enough to understand, and he is at home trying to be a good example for his kids, so that they can look up to him. He is someone that needs a job. He wants a job he can feel good about and make his kids proud.

If our end goal is to stabilize Black families, and this should be our goal, we need to empower men to be men. We need our men back at home. We need them in their role as head of the household. Two parent households are typically more stable. The children are more cared for and well centered and grounded. Most men want to be providers for their families. They relate their manhood to their ability to provide. A certain amount of that is healthy. Young men learn from their Dad's whether he is there or not; but when the Dad is not at home, and is not part of the family, it certainly is not all good.

We want jobs we can feel good about.

Chapter 7

We Want to Feel Empowered

Whether it's true or not, we want to feel like we are the authors of our own destiny. We want to feel empowered; we want to feel like we are valued. We want a seat at the table. Many of us feel that no matter what we do, and how well we do it, we will never be important in our world.

For us, empowerment looks like housing that we can feel good about; and, a Job we can make the ends come close to meeting. Also, empowerment to us means healthcare we can afford and schools that do more than warehouse our kids. We want to feel like a positive contribution to society and this great nation. We want to count for more than the census.

You know that feeling when you get home at the end of the day, and you sigh with relief? You're just glad to be home? We want that. We don't need a mansion. It doesn't matter if it's a house or an apartment, or even a room for rent. But, we want it in safe neighborhoods; where we don't have to fight our way in and out. We want it clean and maintained. I don't mean a pool house or spa; I mean no pest or vermin, basically up to code.

We want jobs we can feel good about. Too many of our Black men through ineffective welfare policies, racism, and the unaddressed psychological baggage have been stripped of their self respect and dignity. They have resorted to alternate means of fulfilling their needs; and, these alternative ways are not beneficial for any of our communities. Our Black men need jobs they can feel good about. They want to feel viable again, so that they feel they have something to contribute to their families and our communities. We need to make our men whole again, so that they can retake their rightful place as the head of the family.

We want healthcare we can afford, and one that makes sense. We want to be able to see a doctor and get our prescriptions. We want insurance that helps us not hurts us; where we have options we can choose that are actually best for us and not the insurance company.

We want educational options for our children. We know education is the key to our future. We want to be able to send our children to school and have them safe and educated.

We want the same things you do.

Part III

What we need

If you give a man a fish you feed him for a day but if you teach him how to fish you feed him for a lifetime.

It's time to go fishing.

Pastor Shannon Wright

Chapter 8

Educational Resources

Until you put in as much time, energy, and resources to ensure the proper education of Blacks, which is proportionate to the amount of time Blacks were denied education, you cannot expect Blacks to achieve the same level of academic success as those who receive the proper education.

We can learn, and we can close this gap. We just need schools that can take into account some of the missing pieces; we need schools that can give what our kids may be missing at home.

Reduce Teen Pregnancy

Children of teenage parents are at greater risk of dropping out of school and leading unsuccessfully or difficult lives. Junior and senior high schools with a high teen pregnancy rates need to implement data driven pregnancy prevention programs. As much as I would like to see abstinence only programs, statistics show that they don't work as well alone as when paired with other approaches.

This is a component I would like to see Churches involved in as well. Sunday worship is great, but we need to call our houses of faith based worship to actively help, and be involved in the community as an act of service in addition to their weekly services. Getting Churches involved in a non-judgmental way would allow them to practice what they preach.

Parent- Training for Low Income or At-Risk Teen Parents

As we require drivers to complete a driver's education course, teen parents should be required to successfully complete an in-person parenting education course. This course would aim at increasing the chances that from Day One, parents will have the tools to be good parents. Also, full effort should be expended to ensure that high-quality parenting education is highly accessible, especially to pregnant teens in low-income locales. In addition, it will be necessary to also develop true innovations in message delivery systems.

Head Start

Logic suggests that a good head start (largely parent-run preschool education), when run according to best practice models, is of significant benefit to a child.

However, successful programs that are to be of significant benefit must be more than babysitting or being a warehouse for children waiting for parents to take them home. They must actually nurture and teach the children the age appropriate skills they may not be getting at home.

Better Trained Teachers

Pre-K to 12 grade, teachers are usually trained mostly in theory-oriented academics. Therefore, teachers are not ready to teach pre-K to grade-12 classrooms, let alone be masters in teaching. This must change. The primary instructors of would-be teachers should be master K-12 teachers, including those who have produced excellent results in educating heavily Black classes and schools.

Teachers of mostly Black classes need to be experts at motivation in addition to their education. This skill set is far beyond what is taught in most teacher education programs. The multicultural education course should include master-teacher-taught lessons on the art of classroom management, including strategies to be effective in working with low-income Black students. Training should not end with the teacher getting their license to teach. Teachers must be supported. In other words, teachers experiencing frustration should be able to phone or email a hotline staffed by teachers who have successfully taught in heavily Black classes and schools.

Flex Classes

It is too much of a challenge for teachers teaching a very wide range of kids in the same class (those who achieve very high grades and those who get very low grades), and trying to accommodate very slow learners and very fast learners, can be a difficult, if not impossible, challenge. The answer is *flex classes*. For academic subjects, it is best to group classes by achievement level, but conduct frequent reviews to ensure that all students, especially children of color, are given the opportunity to move up (or down), as appropriate to their learning needs.

Dispel the Belief: Working Hard is "Acting White"

Many black students believe that being studious is "acting white," and therefore is not cool. We need to change that. Both peers and adults, who are studious, must dispel this myth. One of the best ways to do this is to include, and hire more Black teachers. Another way to solve the problem is to bring successful Blacks from the community, and business leaders, into the classrooms. They will be our best advocates and role models. They will be able to compellingly convince students, and their parents, that studying hard is equally important for students of all races.

Chronically Disruptive Students Must be Placed in Special Classes

If a student, despite the teacher's best efforts (with help from the principal), continues to disrupt his or her classmates, that child must be moved to a special class taught by someone with special skills in working with such kids. This change when necessary should be done as early as possible. The classes that these students are moved to need to have appropriate resources so the students are sill educated and maybe mainstreamed and matriculated back as soon as possible into a main track. The parents must be included in this process. They must be encouraged to rein in their child which is in the child's best interest. If there is an issue causing the behavior, the parents must be required to participate in creating and implementing an action plan appropriate for the child.

Begin Career Exploration in the 6th Grade

We need to start exposing our children to different career choices and paths in the 6th grade. With dropout rates as high as they are for Black children, too many of our children get through high school with little thought as to what to do next.

Our children need early exposure and exploration so that they know that they too have options and choices. In 6th and 7th grade, we need to bring professionals to classrooms for students to be able to ask questions as a part of their career exploration. By 8th grade, we need to be taking our children out into the community to see even more options. Only by getting our children exposed to a world of options beyond their communities, will we get them and their parents thinking about a future, which includes college as a necessity and not optional.

Give Our Kids a Choice: College-Prep or Career-Prep

In the name of high standards, all students, even high school students, who read no better than a 6th grader, can still improve. Instead, students with the ability to work with their hands, are being forced to take college-prep classes in subjects they have no hope of relating to like, quadratic equations. In some states, you cannot get a high school diploma without passing a special exam based on a college prep curriculum. Not surprisingly, this causes a lot of students to drop out rather than wait and be embarrassed by flunking out. If they do graduate and attend college, the dropout rate is even higher. If they manage to defy the odds and graduate from college, they are likely to join the ranks of the countless people with a bachelor's degree stuck in a low-paying job barely better than they would have gotten with a high school diploma. In addition, they get a large debit from huge student loans they have to take out in order to fund their education. Many of these students suffer an ongoing assault to self-esteem from being forced to study academic material for which they have not been prepared for

All students, especially Black students, in junior high and high schools should be offered a *high-quality* career-prep as well as college-prep curriculum. As a parent of Black children, I know not all have the same skill sets and aptitudes. If I had a son or daughter who, through grade 7, showed clear signs of not being likely to succeed in a college-prep curriculum, I'd encourage him or her to choose a career-prep program, especially one with an entrepreneurial component.

Course in Life Skills

Before requiring our at-risk kids and maybe all children to learn simultaneous equations, the halide series of chemical elements, and the use of the doppelganger, students should be required to pass a class in life skills. For example, a life skills course would include topics and subjects in interpersonal communication, budgeting, sex education, and parenting education.

In the life skills course, we need to include a component of character development with ethics thrown in for good measure. Again to close the numerous gaps, we need to give our Black children in Abott or other such underperforming districts the tools necessary to become productive members of society. We need to fill in the things they may not be getting at home. Again this is another area to involve the faith based community.

Try Bold Pilot Studies

The previous proposals are not revolutionary. They are merely some of the best prospects. We should also be pilot testing bold new ideas. For example, one commenter suggested sending our Black kids to deeply impoverished parts of the World, perhaps as part of the

White Folks Guide to Understanding the Black Community

Peace Corps, in hopes that such a journey would inspire them. Here are a few other out-of-the-box ideas:

- Pair at-risk kids with nursing home residents or hard-to-adopt animal-shelter dogs and cats who otherwise would be euthanized. Doing this helps kids have a chance to come out of their comfort zones in a non-threatening way. By working with senior citizens, the kids will have a chance to feel as if they have a extended family, which they may be lacking at home. It also would give them a sounding board to express ideas, thoughts, and concerns that they can't express at home. Also, when it comes to working with animals, our kids would have a chance to be responsible. The experience could even serve as an introduction to parenting and family classes by teaching them how to be responsible for another living thing.
- Introduce kids to planting vegetables and fruits, cooking, and eating what they grow,   and how to sell the rest. They will learn science, cooking, nutrition, and how to run a business.
- Create peer- mentoring pairs both up and down. Pair at-risk 6th graders with at-risk 1st graders and up with at-risk 12th graders. Pair at-risk 12th graders also with adults. This way you create a chain of learning and responsibility. Am I my brother's keeper? Yes, yes I am.

I have continued to focus a lot in this book on education and learning. I do this because I believe education and learning are keys to success. If we can steer our kids in the right direction, and teach them the things they need to know to be successful in school, at home, and in the community, we will see our children become successful in life.

Chapter 9

Education Is More than Books, Bricks, and Mortar

To help me you need to know me. You would not go into an AP class and teach those students remedial work. The same applies here.

The first step would be to convert all low performing, title 1, and former Abbot Schools to community charter schools. All schools would have the right components to be active participants in the community including faith based involvement. Understand this is *something that can be done now on the State level without any need for Federal legislative intervention. This is something that would from day 1 save the taxpayers' money, since charter schools are funded at 80% of public schools.*

By creating more charter schools, public schools would be forced to improve in order to compete for students. Competition would force unions to be open to change and compromise, as well as allowing teachers room to teach. This change would force public schools to improve in order to keep their rosters and funding.

Plus, charter schools have an inherent ability to be more flexible. I believe they have the best ability to educate our children.

The following are excerpts from our actual Charter school application being submitted October 2012 for fastrack.

Part 1: Program and Operations Plan

1. Mission, Vision, and Educational Philosophy

The mission of the Fredrick Douglas Academy for Leadership and Social Change is to ignite in every student the wonder of learning, and to provide meaningful and educational experiences. In our academy, we create a challenging, learning environment that encourages high expectations for success through development-appropriate instruction that allows for individual differences and learning styles. Our school is an influential force in developing the next generation of leaders in a safe, orderly, caring, and supportive environment. Each student's self-esteem is fostered by positive relationships with students and staff. We create a school community that mirrors the best functioning societal community by fostering bonds and open communication. We create a positive and supportive environment, where students, parents, teachers, and community members are actively involved in our students' learning growth and development.

White Folks Guide to Understanding the Black Community

The Fredrick Douglas Academy for Leadership and Social Change is committed to realizing its mission by providing:

- Strong standards-based academics
- Accelerated instruction based on the students' own capacity and pace
- An enriched curriculum through exposure to a foreign language (Spanish, Chinese, Russian, Japanese, Arabic, German, etc...)
- Real world mentors based on personal and professional interests
- Cultural immersion through classes, programs, workshops, trips, and community interaction)

As our theme is leadership and social change, a well rounded understanding of tolerance and cultural diversity is essential to our success. We will include the following as a part of our instruction for all levels:

- Promote the elimination of discrimination.
- Promote mutual acceptance, respect among students, and enable students to interact effectively with others regardless of race, national origin, sexual orientation, gender, religion, English proficiency, socio-economic status or disability.
- Provide instruction in multicultural education content and practices.

- Provide instruction in African-American History as part of U.S. History.
- Provide instruction on the Holocaust and genocide.

We chose our district of residence because there is a serious need in Plainfield, and because the area combines an area of intense academic need with an area of intense community support and involvement. Charter schools succeed when they are built on a solid foundation of academic excellence, parental involvement, and community commitment. A solid foundation in schools, and the community, helps students gain real world experiences, and students can then become well equipped future leaders.

The specific theme of the Fredrick Douglas Academy for Leadership and Social Change is cultural diversity and tolerance. The academy has a strong commitment to the development of leaders. The academy's objective is to equip students with the necessary tools to successfully handle the challenges that lay before them. Its dedication is to develop a generation of doctors, lawyers, and teachers; leaders that are ready to lead. Students that have a well-rounded base of solid academics, and cultural sensitivity on a global perspective are ready to handle the challenges of the 21st century.

4. Student Populations

Special Education/Gifted Education

At The Frederick Douglas Academy for Leadership and Social Justice Charter School, special education services will be available to exceptional children, including both students with disabilities and gifted students, in accordance with New Jersey State Law *N.J.A.C. 6A:14-1.* Within the scope of the educational program, defined by The Frederick Douglas Academy for Leadership and Social Justice Charter School, the school does not discriminate based on ability or disability. Accommodations for students will be made by following the principles outlined in, *Teaching Special Education Students in the Regular Classroom*, and *Teaching the Talented and Gifted in the Regular Classroom,* by Susan Winebrenner (other recommended resources will be used as well).

Students at The Frederick Douglas Academy for Leadership and Social Justice Charter School can expect to be challenged and to work hard. All students will be expected to master basic skills and content, as well as higher-order thinking skills and concepts. The Academy will have elementary school teachers that will be experienced in, and committed to, providing rich and challenging experiences in the classroom. The middle and high school teachers will demonstrate a high level of knowledge in their content areas, and they will have excellent teaching strategies. Teachers will use performance grouping within the class as appropriate (grades K-5). The placement in core courses will determine mastery of previous material and aptitude (grades 6-12) in order to meet the needs of students.

In addition to regular classroom teachers, the school will employ a resource teacher with certification in special education and experience in classroom differentiation strategies for exceptional children. The resource teacher will work with students, classroom teachers, and parents to identify and develop additional strategies for meeting the needs of students with diverse learning styles. The resource teacher will also work with teachers to implement a program incorporating study skills in the classroom to benefit all students. Additional special education services will be provided by specialists in accordance with a student's Individual Education Plan (IEP).

Limited-English Proficient Students

Since the systematic separation of limited-English proficient (LEP) students from the mainstream in bilingual programs has the ultimate effect of isolating such students, the school will consistently place as many LEP students as possible in the regular classes. This approach practices inclusion. It also recognizes the immersion method of language acquisition as the fastest, most complete, and most effective. In addition, it is a method which is eminently suitable for children who may learn as much language from interaction with playmates as from formal instruction. For students whose English language proficiency is so limited as to prevent them from following most of the activities in a regular classroom, the school will provide instruction in English as a second language for a certain period of time every day at school. Because the objective is to transition the students to mainstream English classes, the LEP students will also be expected to participate, partially at first, in the regular classroom schedule, where they will have the opportunity to hear and use English. Evaluation of such children for English language proficiency will occur at least annually, but more frequently if the child's progress warrants. Provisions will then be made to communicate with the students' parents.

If 20 or more LEP students, who speak the same language and qualify for a bilingual program, are enrolled at The Frederick Douglas Academy for Leadership and Social Justice Charter School, we will provide a high intensity ESL program developed in conjunction with the State Department of Education per state guidelines and pursuant to *N.J.A.C. 6:31-1.5*. The Frederick Douglas Academy for Leadership and Social Justice Charter School has requested a waiver of the requirement for a bilingual program based on the improbability of sufficient enrollment of such students; please refer to Section 15Waivers of Regulations.

At-Risk Students

The Frederick Douglas Academy for Leadership and Social Justice Charter School will develop and apply consistently a procedure to identify and educate at-risk students. In all instances, this procedure will adhere to all student protection, parent consent and notification requirements, and due process provisions of the relevant statutes and applicable regulations.

At-risk students may exhibit one or more of the following characteristics: failure to perform at the specified grade-level in one or more subject areas, poor school attendance, limited English proficiency, disruptive or disaffected behavior, a history of behavioral problems, or pregnant and, or dealing with unplanned parenthood.

Students will be identified as potentially at-risk by the teachers in the course of daily classroom observations and assessments of pupil performance and behavior; or, students will be identified by their parents, or guardians, who communicate their concerns to the Frederick Douglas Academy for Leadership and Social Justice Charter School staff.

The Frederick Douglas Academy for Leadership and Social Justice Charter School supports at-risk students by following the prevention, intervention, and improved learning environment approach, which is outlined in *NJAC 6:8-6.2*. Many features of the regular school environment and curriculum promote an atmosphere, which minimizes the need for interventions. These include general approaches, such as, recognition of a variety of learning and teaching styles and encouragement of active parental involvement for improved home-school communication; as well as, specific curriculum items, such as, conflict resolution or substance abuse in health. The Frederick Douglas Academy for Leadership and Social Justice Charter School maintains a safe, disciplined school atmosphere, which encourages learning.

Although the emphasis of the Frederick Douglas Academy for Leadership and Social Justice Charter School education program is for the prevention of great academic problems, integrated assessments allow for immediate intervention in the case of insufficient achievement. Thus, students identified with having difficulties receive individual tutoring during the daily reading period. If this proves to be insufficient, additional time will be scheduled for tutoring in reading, writing and basic mathematics, or in other subjects as needed.

The Frederick Douglas Academy for Leadership and Social Justice Charter School recognizes that some of the at-risk student difficulties may be due to health or emotional problems and/or to the family's circumstances. The Frederick Douglas Academy for Leadership and Social Justice Charter School will maintain an up-to-date list of social and health service agencies and organizations at the local and state level. The school will refer students and/,or their families to such agencies or organizations when appropriate; and the school will follow up each case and act as an advocate for the student and family.

Although every effort will be made to mitigate factors causing a pupil to be academically at risk, in some cases, this may not be possible. In case of such continuing difficulties, a

Pupil Assistance Committee constituted per state guidelines, and with the consent of parents/guardians, will conduct an evaluation of the student. In a joint meeting, parents, the classroom teacher, and the PAC will develop a written plan of action for the at-risk student. For students who fail to benefit from this plan, a child study team will determine the eligibility of the child for special education and determine his/her classification. Within no more than 30 days, the child- study team will work out an individualized education program (IEP), and within another 30 days that program will begin to be implemented. The student will be reevaluated upon recommendations from either the teachers, child study team, or by the parents/guardians, but no later than within three years.

Parental Involvement

The Frederick Douglas Academy for Leadership and Social Justice Charter School offers three avenues for parent involvement in the school: through the governance structure, both on the board of trustees and the standing and ad hoc committees, through volunteer activities, and through the daily involvement of parents monitoring their children's academic progress. Parental involvement manifests itself at the highest level in the governance structure of The Frederick Douglas Academy for Leadership and Social Justice Charter School, since parents constitute the majority of the Board of Trustees. In addition, both Trustee and non-Trustee parents may serve on Board advisory committees.

Parents may also establish committees under their own initiative to enrich the life of the school. These committees may undertake a number of school-wide projects such as book fairs, school picnics, after-school clubs, community service, and other activities. At least two room parents will be secured for each class in the school serving as liaisons between the classroom teacher and other parents.

Parents will be involved in the school on a daily basis by supporting their children's academic endeavors. For example, they may be requested to initial their children's homework assignments to ensure the timely completion of homework. Not only will The Frederick Douglas Academy for Leadership and Social Justice Charter School communicate with parents openly and frequently about their children's progress, but the Academy will also keep them informed about the school as a whole, during open houses, orientations, and back-to-school nights. A collection of the textbooks, and other books used by the students, will be maintained in the office, and these books will be easily accessible to parents. Parents will be asked to give their view of their child's academic progress guided by a questionnaire to be developed by a joint parent-teacher committee. Parents who choose not to submit a written evaluation will be offered the opportunity to have a personal interview.

Community Group Involvement

The Princeton area is home to experts in many disciplines. Such community resources, and partnerships between The

Frederick Douglas Academy for Leadership and Social Justice Charter School may enrich the school's educational program. For example, a local astronomer might prepare materials to supplement the school's textbooks in the event of a significant astronomical discovery. In all cases, such materials will be subject to the approval and quality assurance process, which will be applied to all the Frederick Douglas Academy for Leadership and Social Justice Charter School instructional materials. A disciplined approach to the production of such materials through partnerships is an interesting objective in its own right. The Frederick Douglas Academy for Leadership and Social Justice Charter School may seek outside funding for such projects.

Many organizations have been contacted and are considering what their level of involvement will be in the development of the Frederick Douglas Academy for Leadership and Social Justice Charter School arts program.

Representatives of the Founders have contacted a range of local organizations, and community groups, to inform them about the plans for a charter school and to learn about their interests in and ideas on education. Central New Jersey has a diverse population, and the Founders of the Frederick Douglas Academy for Leadership and Social Justice Charter School believe it is important to reach out to all the segments of the community.

The Frederick Douglas Academy for Leadership and Social Justice Charter School Founders will continue this outreach effort by setting up public meetings to explain the mission, goals, and admissions process of The Frederick Douglas Academy for Leadership and Social Justice Charter School. They will seek out all those who are interested in helping constructively with the work of forming a school.

As I said in the beginning, these are excerpts from our actual application for a charter school in New Jersey. We did a lot of research on how to educate Black children in a way that is not only effective, but cost effective as well. We named the school The Frederick Douglas Academy for Leadership and Social Justice because Frederick Douglas was a very important part of our Black history.

Frederick Douglass was someone who had stood for LIFE-EMPOWERING values (such as):

(1) Respect for the Constitution

(2) Respect for Life

(3) Belief in Limited Government

(4) Belief in Personal Responsibility

Having served as the catalyst within the Abolitionist Movement, which was an integral part of our nation's history and ended slavery, Douglass' political views align with the beliefs of the Founding Fathers.

The name Frederick Douglas is one of many that the Black community has had respect for. He is known to have been a key figure in both Black history and American history in general. He believed in, and personified, the views, goals, and philosophies that we look to unstill in our Black children. For that reason, we chose to identify our program with his name and make it a program that could stand well in any minority community. The issues with educating our Black children are national, and the key part of the solution is—The Frederick Douglas Academy for Leadership and Social Justice Charter School national program.

Chapter 10

Tying Education Together

The key to a successful education environment is a healthy partnership between parents, educators, students, and the community. We need to teach parents how to educate their children. Most parents know they need to make sure their children go to school and may even ask the child if they have homework. Few go beyond that. We need to teach parents the steps to insure they are raising well educated children.

We need to open up more options for parents in low performing districts and show them how to find the best options for their child. The ideal situation would be a choice between charter schools or voucher schools. Charter schools should be the first option. Charter schools keep resources in the community and actually bring in more resources. However, if there are no spaces available in charter schools then parents should be able to use vouchers for a school of their choice. Parents need options.

In all of my research, there is one thing that I see that seems to be having immediate positive results, and long range implications, and that is urban debate

Pastor Shannon Wright

clubs. I would institute a debate (forensics) program in all title 1 high schools, including those with low achievement scores. There's some data (and a lot of common sense) to suggest that this could yield significant long and short term benefits. Think and work smart. Inspire other thinkers; challenge them to create the solutions to the problems they see every day. Inspire the children to be the think tank that finds the solution.

WHY DEBATE?
Thanks to the National Association for Urban Debate Leagues (www.naudl.org), who have recorded every study relating to the academic benefits of debate, the following quotations are from their studies (a few are quotes from former debaters).

"Those 4 years in debate were the educational foundation of everything I did. And I don't mean that in some simple form...I'm saying the finest education I got from any of the institutions I attended, the foundation of my mind that I got during those 4 years of competitive policy debate."

- John Sexton, President of New York University

"Maybe you could be a mayor or a Senator or a Supreme Court Justice, but you might not know that until you join student government or the debate team."

- President Barack Obama

"I think debating in high school and college is most valuable training whether for politics, the law, business, or for service... A good debater must not only study material in support of his own case, but he must also, of course, thoroughly analyze the expected argument of his opponent. The give and take of debating, the testing of ideas, is essential to democracy."

- President John F. Kennedy

"Standing up there, the faces looking up at me, the things in my head coming out of my mouth, while my brain searched for the next best thing to follow what I was saying, and if I could sway them to my side by handling it right, then I had won the debate--once my feet got wet, I was gone on debating."

- Malcolm X

"it is the greatest good for a human being to have discussions every day about virtue and the other things you hear me talking about, examining myself and others, and that the unexamined life is not livable for a human belng."

- Socrates (*The Republic* by Plato)

CRITICAL THINKING

The kind of oppositional thinking encouraged by debate helps to develop critical thinking skills. There is strong evidence that using a devil's advocacy philosophy helps improve the understanding of strategic problems. Debaters learn about critical thinking, and the old adage, "there are two sides to every coin." They learn how to spot errors in reasoning and proof. They gain respect for the complexity of ideas and learn how to criticize in a productive way based on facts and logic. James Greenwood, Chairperson in Communications at the University of Findlay noted that, "debate was more important to my career than any single course on the undergraduate and graduate level. Debate develops skills in organization, clarity and depth of analysis that most students do not encounter until the master's thesis."

COLLEGE ADMISSIONS

Too many of our Black students have parents who did not go to college and friends that won't even graduate from high school. However, more than 75% of urban debaters go to four-year colleges. Urban Debate Leagues produce college matriculation rates around 80%. Debate will give our Black students the tools and connections to succeed in college. The students will compete and research on college campuses, receive coaching from college students, and debate in front of college recruiters. This exposure to the college environment will raise the debater's expectations, and give him or her a sense that getting into best colleges in America is an obtainable goal.

White Folks Guide to Understanding the Black Community

LEADERSHIP

Debate programs prepare students to become leaders in their communities. Debaters are represented in leadership ranks in law, business, and academics. With more opportunity, and by learning to lead and compete, urban debaters are equipped to improve their schools, strengthen their communities, and ultimately broaden the local and national leadership base. A survey by the National Forensic League shows that 64% of the Members of the United States Congress competed in debate or speech in high school.

EQUALITY

*Urban Debate Leagues (*UDLs) promote education equity. They provide rigorous academic training to students from all across participating cities. Some of the urban public school students then go on to compete nationally and win. UDLs have placed highly at state debate championships in California, Georgia, Illinois, New Jersey, and New York. They are debunking the myth that our Black students lack the ability to articulate clearly. UDL teams have been in the top 16 National Finalists on four separate occasions.

ACADEMIC RIGOR

Policy debate is the most academically rigorous and widely used of all interscholastic speech activities. It is also the oldest, dating back to 1928, of all high school academic competitions. Policy debate develops core academic skills in literacy, critical thinking, research, communication, and organization.

CAREER READINESS

The knowledge economy demands that high schools equip graduates have the skills necessary for post-secondary success. Urban Debate Leagues have been shown to increase college and career readiness.

Preparing students for professional careers is important. Debate alumni overwhelmingly agree that debate experience has aided them significantly in their professional careers. In general, it seems that training in debate provides students with a positive experience, which helps them to develop skills they will need in their professions. Several students, in response to the open-ended questions, said debate was the most valuable educational experience they have received. One minister wrote, "The most useful training I received in college for the ministry came from my experience in debate. Period."

INCREASING GRADUATION RATES

Raising the percentage of Black students in urban schools, that graduate from high school, is a challenge.

White Folks Guide to Understanding the Black Community

There are many issues to take into consideration. Urban Debate Leagues have been shown to raise on-time graduation rates and decrease drop-out rates for students.

AFRICAN AMERICAN MALES

In a study of the Chicago Debate League, Black male students raised their GPAs by 50% of a letter grade and were 70% more likely to graduate from high school than non-debating Black males. Compared to their non-debating students, Black male debaters were 70% more likely to reach the ACT College Ready benchmark in Reading, and were twice as likely to reach the College Ready benchmark in English.

GRADE IMPROVEMENT

According to the Director of the Chicago Debate League, the sample of 76 urban debaters and 37 comparison group students were drawn from five Chicago Public Schools high schools and represented students across all four years in school. The results show that during the study period, urban debaters improved their grades by 7.6% (average GPA went from 3.17 to 3.41); in contrast to the comparison group, whose grades fell 1.3% (average GPA went from 2.98 to 2.94). The second study consisted of 59 urban debaters and 34 comparison group students, and again the students were drawn from five Chicago public high schools, which represented students from all four school years. This study concluded that urban debaters improved their grades from the Spring of 1998 to the Spring of 1999 by 6.6% (average GPA went from 3.31 to 3.52); this was compared to a comparison group, whose grades went down 0.7% (average GPA went from 3.03 to 3.01).

IMPROVING LITERACY RATES

On average students increased their reading comprehension by more than 3 grade levels after 1 year in debate. Students who debated for more than 1 year performed more than a full grade level higher than controls. Even students who improve their basic literacy skills in earlier grades, often don't advance beyond basic literacy.

IMPROVING SELF ESTEEM

A study assessed students involved in debates. The study concentrated on how debates impact reading, self-esteem, and risk-taking behaviors in urban high school students. A group of 209 debaters and a comparison group of 212 urban high school students participated. The students were drawn from urban high school students in five cities across the country. A standardized reading test, the Scholastic Reading Inventory, was given in a pre-test/post-test format, with a self-report survey of risk-taking behavior. The study showed that, "academic debate improves performance at statistically significant levels on reading test scores, diminishes high-risk behaviors, and improves academic success and student attitudes towards higher education." Linda Collier at the University of Missouri, Kansas City, led the research team. Data analysis was conducted by Elaine Maag of the Urban Institute and Edward Harris of the Congressional Budget Office. Notable findings include:

◦ There was a 25% increase in debater (n=209) reading scores compared to the increase in the control (entire n=212) category scores. Debaters increased test scores 18% more than the honors controls (n=64).
◦ "The fall results combined with the very significant difference in the arts results predicts positive academic results and lower behavior risk for debaters.
◦ "The spring scores reflect a statistically significant increase in GPA by debaters over controls."
◦ Linda Collier suggests that, "this study shows that debate uses competition to motivate increased reading — a basic and essential building block of education — in a powerful way that will help students for the rest of their lives."

(Arguments for Success: A Study of Academic Debate in the Urban High Schools of Chicago, Kansas City, New York, St. Louis, and Seattle (2004).)

IMPROVING TITLE I SCHOOLS

Secretary of Education, Arne Duncan, has made it a priority to improve our lowest-performing schools. The Urban Debate League focuses on these schools. They provide students with chances to learn and they help low performing schools have a chance to raise the ceiling.

IMPROVING TEST SCORES

Both quantitative and qualitative methods were used to collect data for this study using a pre-test/post-test protocol. For a more accurate outcome, researchers recruited a set of comparison students to participate in the testing alongside the debater cohort. Scholastic Reading Inventory materials were used along with a survey to get background characteristics. students' report of academic performance, school attendance, involvement in academic and debate activities; attitudes, such as interest in school and intention to attend college; locus of control; self-esteem; reasons for joining the UDL; and the Adolescent Risk Taking Scale. (These tests were given in the fall of 2004 and spring of 2005). School records provided students' GPAs, English classes taken, academic progress (age for grade, school promotion), school attendance, and eligibility for free or reduced-price lunch. The results were:

◦ Debaters scored 36% higher on the reading post-test than on the pre-test. This improvement is 61% greater than improvements among the comparison group.

○ 80% of debaters reported no attendance problems compared to 49.02% with no reported attendance problems among the comparison group.

○ Debaters averaged 15% higher self-esteem than the comparison group, and this boost in self-esteem was positively correlated with the duration of debate participation: the longer he/she debated, the wider the differential.

○ By the end of their first year of debate, 100% of the debaters reported an increased interest in their classes.

○ Compared to the comparison group, 87% of debaters were better able to analyze information.

○ On a 4.0 scale, the gross average of debaters' 2006 GPAs was 2.97, compared to 2.5875 among the comparison group. Returning debaters averaged a 0.13 increase in their GPAs, while returning comparison group members lost an average of 0.10 points.

○ 100% of Minneapolis UDL debaters were unlikely to engage in negative risk behavior (drug use, early pregnancy, and alcohol). Debaters scored the highest possible score on this indicator.

(*The Effect of the Minnesota Urban Debate League on the Academic and Social Development Outcomes of Students, First Year Report (2005).*)

CLOSING THE CIVICS ACHIEVEMENT GAP

The academic achievement gap has received the most press attention, but, for several reasons, the civics achievement gap is even a greater threat to America's future. First, the civics achievement gap has received very little attention and solutions. Second, citizenship, an informed electorate, and political participation are essential to a democratic republic. When we lack these elements, we cannot truly call ourselves a democracy.

*   *   *

Parents need options. A well run education system that is actually educating our Black children is critical to our future as a culture, and society. It is critical to our nation as a whole.

Until we put resources into educating Black children in direct proportion to the amount of time we were denied education and in many cases are still not able to get quality public education, you cannot expect our children to be able to close the education or civics gap. Title 1 and Abott were both intended to close the gap. They did not succeed. As with most things, in order to get the best, you need to introduce competition. The same goes for education. We must make the public schools compete to keep the dollars they covet.

In many cases, taxpayers complain greatly about the amount of their tax dollars going to education, especially considering how many schools are failing our children. We need education tax reform. Just as we need to give parents options, we need to give taxpayers options as well. Since you don't have a choice in that you have to pay property tax, you should have a choice of where you want to pay it to. What if your properly tax bill was $10,000 and you opted to have your taxes go to a low performing school and got 150% credit on your taxes? Would you do it? What if, as a part of education reform, we also had education funding reform? Abott and Title 1 may be mandated but there is discretion in the funding process. Why not give taxpayers a choice too?

Chapter 11

Leaders and Role Models

The mainstream media has gone awry when it comes to who the Leaders of the Black Community are. Instead of focusing on the positive and good, people of color, they have chosen to focus on the more flamboyant, racist, twisted minded, and whoever can scream the loudest.

Even the so - called Conservative media like "Fox News" seem to give people like Jesse Jackson, Al Sharpton, and the New Black Panther Party, more of a forum, rather than Conservative Blacks like Allan West, Herman Cain, or CL Bryant. The only time you will hear from the Black Conservatives it seems, is when the Left is slinging mud and they are forced to try and defend themselves. Usually even then, they only get a little time in a segment that was only given due to a negative thing coming out against them.

I don't know when AL Sharpton and Jesse Jackson became the leader of the black Community for the United States. I do know that there has never been a vote, a show of hands, or even a poll for this justification; and if there was I must have been absent or sick that day.

Alfred Charles Sharpton Jr. (Better known as Al Sharpton,) is known for being a Baptist Minister and Civil Rights Activist. The same could be said of Jesse Louis Burns, (who is better known as the Reverend Jesse Jackson). Both made names for themselves during the Civil Rights Movement during the 1960s. Both are very vocal in their views on Equality and Racism, and have made it their life's voicing and stomping out racial inequalities in our Country.

The New Black Panther Party was founded in 1989 by Malik Zulu Shabazz (Paris Lewis), who is an attorney and its National Chairman. The New Black Panther Party caused a bit of confusion because the original Black Panther Party, founded in 1966 by Huey Newton and Bobby Seale, holds that there isn't a New Black Panther Party and that the NBPP is illegitimate. Whichever way the chips may fall, legitimate or not, the Panthers have always been known for their Racist antics and tirades in the media. They have also made a name for themselves with their use of violence, their militaristic style, and their hand jester "Black Power" symbolizing the Black Power Movement.

The persons the media chooses to focus on and promote are all the wrong people!!! I do understand that ratings and numbers is how they make their money but at what cost and whose expense? Let's face the facts folks. AL and Jesse can find racism in a pickle jar and the Black Panther Party is just a group of unintelligent, free loading, racists. These people are using their own community to line their own pockets, not caring who they hurt in the process.

The use of the media outlets, be it Television, Music, Newspaper or Blog sensation, does nothing to help in understanding the Black Community nor does it help in making things better for anyone. Sharpton, Jackson and the

Original Black Panther Party were indeed an asset back in the 60's and 70's but is the same radical ideology needed now? And is it truly necessary to put them in the limelight every time they say something? Did you ever think that maybe you are putting the wrong Black people in the limelight?

Are these really the people that should be viewed by the general population as the leaders of an entire community? I think not. The media tends to glorify the wrong things and the wrong people. By showing a stereotype, the media in all formats, keeps racial division and racism alive. The media teaches that all blacks are uneducated, gang members, drug dealers, welfare recipients, and other various things. They may not see it that way, but they do. When you see black people in movies it's usually a role of a gang banger, criminal, drug user, rapper, or drug dealer. Those that they show in a good light are still shown in a negative connotation.

Take Bill Cosby and his television series for example. The Cosby Show was one of the few shows that showed blacks as being successful, educated, goal and family orientated, that also incorporate real-life lessons into its programming. At the same time, the media then chooses to run news stories about Bill Cosby and how other popular Blacks disagree with his viewpoints and politics. They are quick to point out that he makes statements that criticized the Black Communities and the prioritization of the Black Communities' values. People in the media have called Bill

Cosby "out of touch" and racial slurs like "Uncle Tom" and a "sellout".

The media, in all its different forums, shapes the way people see the world. The majority of Americans today are not rocket scientists. They use the media to get their news, fashion trends, and other things they put to use in their everyday lives. If we can change the media perception and negative connotations of the Black Community, then the Black Community will also change. It won't happen overnight, but it will change.

The media in all its forms should look for and choose to focus on Blacks who are positive in the community if they truly need to put forth a leader of the Black Community. A few good ones are: Alan Keyes, Hermain Cain, Deborah Honeyailt, Condolayza Rice, CL Bryant, Erika Harold, Virginia Feeler, J.C. Watts, Michael Steele, Star Parker, Bill Cosby, Angela McGlowan, Stephen Broden, Joseph C. Phillips, Lynn Swan, Karl Malone, Armstrong Williams, James Earl Jones, Mia Love, 50 Cent, Cow Boy Troy, Olveda King, Keith Butler, Peter Bolware; Sheryl Underwood, T.D. Jakes, Will Chamberlain, Clarence Thomas, Yaphet Kotto, Duane Johnson, David Tyree, Thurman Thomas, LL Cool J, Lloyd Marcus, and many more.

If you noticed, I've listed prominent Blacks who are Republicans. I did that on purpose because most do not know that there are many Black Republicans. The media would have you believe that Black Conservatives and Black Republicans are a myth, and that simply is not true. The media would focus on how Black Republicans and Conservatives are ostracized by their own community rather than the reasons they are ostracized. The media plays a big part in the ostracizing of Blacks within their own community. The media has made the label "too white" and promoted it heavily in TV, print, and in our music.

When I was growing up, my great-grandmother was very strict when it came to education and being a proper person. I had no idea that speaking proper English, working hard to achieve my goals, and not expecting everything to be handed to me would get me classified as being "too white" or as a "sellout" as many like to call me these days.

If you ask a grade school black child what being too white is, they will tell you things like: Someone who is black but is rich, a black person who speaks proper English, a black person who stays in school, a black person who doesn't hang out with other blacks, a black person who doesn't speak the same as they do, a black person who doesn't like gangs or drugs, a black person who likes white people, a black person who hasn't done anything illegal, a black person who doesn't like black food, a black person who doesn't date other black people, a black person who thinks they are better than they are because they get out of the hood, and the kicker…. a black person who is a Republican. When I asked how they know this, they will say, the TV, name a famous black comedian or rapper that has made the remarks or say their mom or dad says so. I also have been told "Everybody knows this duh…. Even white people."

White Folks Guide to Understanding the Black Community

We must change the image of the Black Community and its so-called leaders in order to fix anything. Because of the negativity brought by the media, the Black Community believes and is told by its so-called leaders they need help and must rely on the government. They teach Whites are responsible for all of their problems. The Black Community has lost its sense of self worth and personal responsibility. Black is seen as bad, unintelligent, and ugly.

Blacks that have found their way off of the Liberal Plantation and don't see their color as a hindrance are ostracized. Blacks see them as sell-outs and race trading. The white community and media doesn't help any. You may think that by making statements such as "I have black friends" and "my friend is a Black Conservative who has come off the Liberal Plantation" is helping; but it really isn't. You now have put race back on the forefront. Instead, try sticking to the facts and the things you have in common. When a conversation's foundation is built on common ground, people tend to keep cooler heads and learn more about each other and what they have in common. Often people will find they have more in common and see eye to eye on things which in turn open dialogue. That dialogue is the first step to changing hearts and minds.

Chapter 12

Healthcare Reform

Few legislative efforts and agendas have caused as much heated debate as The Affordable Healthcare Act. There is impassioned debate on both sides. The supporters of the Act argue that all Americans need and deserve healthcare. The counter argument is that all Americans deserve healthcare, however, it should not be forced to come out of the taxpayers' pockets on the backs of small business.

There are really plausible arguments on both sides. I myself have gone back and forth on this issue. As a parent, I like the aspect of children being able to stay on their parents plan longer. As a daughter of an aging and chronically ill mother, I can appreciate the expansion of a home care system for the chronically ill that would reduce repeated hospital visits for the elderly. The flip side is that, as a small business owner, the additional cost hinders business growth.

But, we come to this question again, "Am I my brother's keeper?" "Yes, I am." As such, are we not responsible, or at least obligated, to spare human life? Taking economics out of the equation, it is the right thing to do. In the Black community, the need for extended healthcare is critical. We need healthcare. Since the Affordable Healthcare Legislation is the current law of the land, with its staggered component rollouts, it is important that we understand the political implications of public consent or dissent. Simply put, many Black folks look at dissent as a conscious choice to let us suffer and in some cases die.

Many states have pilot programs in different stages of development to both meet the mandates of the legislation, and the needs of the communities they serve; these programs are sometimes at cross purposes.

The state of Louisiana has a pilot program that is very interesting. The program is run by the Micah Project and its affiliates and members.

The Micah Project is a faith-based organization established in 2007 by clergy who wanted to see real change in their communities. Micah works with its 16 member congregations to create innovative solutions to the plethora of problems faced by those living in the Greater, New Orleans area. Micah is a member of the PICO National Network, an organization whose mission is to provide families and grassroots leaders with a voice in the decisions that shape their lives and communities, and of PICO, Louisiana, PICO's state-wide chapter. Micah is a non-partisan, non-denominational, multiracial, multicultural collective of clergy and congregations that are united together for a common good (from their site).

Every year, 700,000 people file for bankruptcy due to medical debts. Micah is working to fix this problem and improve healthcare access for everyone. Together with its partners, the Daughters of Charity, Louisiana State University (LSU), Louisiana Public Health Institute (LPHI), and Bayou Health/LA Care, they have initiated a healthcare pilot program to improve health, increase access to primary care, and re-direct ER savings to primary care services.

Through their program, people with chronic diseases, that have been using the ER for all healthcare needs, are linked to primary care providers and a community healthcare team. They help participants get over obstacles that prevent them from getting the care they need to change their health situation. With Micah's community engagement process, including face-to-face interviews, canvassing, and local focus groups, some barriers are being removed for participants seeking healthcare, including transportation, the cost of seeing a provider, and lack of education on how to manage their own chronic condition.

White Folks Guide to Understanding the Black Community

In New Orleans ¼ of the zip codes account for over ½ of the visits to LSU's emergency room. These same zip codes have less than 1/7 of the city's primary care physicians. Hundreds of people have no choice, but to use the ER for primary care needs. This is costing the city money and decreasing quality of life. The new pilot program will target people with chronic manageable diseases, who live in high-ER zip codes, and use the ER for their primary care needs; also, the program is structured to help these patients make necessary changes in their lifestyles and catch problems before they the end up in the emergency room.

I had a conversation with a family friend from Baton Rouge, Louisiana. He has an interest in several healthcare entities in that area. I always like to have political conversations with him. He is always a staunch conservative Republican. Always!!! Through his business interests, he deals with insurance companies and public policy on a daily basis. We were talking about family and got around to politics. He told me horror stories of the people that fall through the cracks of the system. He told me stories of patients who are regulars at the emergency room not because they were critically ill, but chronically ill. For them, the emergency room has become the primary care physician office. He also explained that this problem has been driving up the cost of hospital visits. He explained that it is less expensive to have The Affordable Healthcare Act in place in the long run. One other vital point in the conversation was when he asked me a rhetorical question, "How do you turn away someone who you know will die without care. How do you do that and sleep at night?"

The Louisiana pilot is an interesting concept. Apparently, they tried it with approximately 30,000 patients and are looking to expand to 300,000. The concept I find the most beneficial is the home care portion. They have a home care component that makes home visits to access the whole situation. They access what is causing the patient to not be able to make proper use of the healthcare system, and they work to remove those obstacles. Those patients with multiple chronic illnesses get more monitoring to reduce repeated hospital visits. They have realized a 30% savings so far. The philosophy is that if we can keep you in your home and not in the hospital, the cost is lower and the care is more personal and more accurate.

In researching, Micah I found 2 other programs of interest in New Jersey. One in Camden, New Jersey, named Camden Coalition of Healthcare Providers, and the other in Atlantic City, New Jersey, named the Special Care Center. All 3 programs have some very interesting components.

The Camden Coalition, as it is commonly called, is working to create a broad coalition of stakeholders of businesses, hospitals, healthcare providers, and consumer groups, led by the NJ Chamber of Commerce. They have joined together for the creation of Medicaid Accountable Care Organizations (ACOs) in New Jersey. New legislation (S2443 / A3636) was recently introduced in New Jersey to test the idea in a Medicaid ACO demonstration project. Aligned closely with the ACOs, described in the federal Affordable Care Act, the legislation would create multi-stakeholder, geographic Medicaid ACOs. This group was started by Doctor Jeffrey Brenner.

This group works in urban areas. They are targeting their services to Medicaid patients in urban areas that have a high rate of emergency room visits. These chronically ill, but not critically ill patients drive up medical costs with repeated emergency room visits instead of primary care visits. This programs philosophy is that if you address the needs of the most expensive patients, you undoubtedly find savings by reducing repeat visits and duplication of services. This group started in 2002 as a group of doctors that met fairly regularly to discuss and plan ways of improving health care, while bringing down the cost of that healthcare system. They are now an actual practice, and program.

They work closely with the churches in their area to coordinate their outreach efforts.

The Special Care Center in Atlantic City was also formed to improve health care, while cutting cost. It started as an experiment in 2007 by the health-benefit programs of the casino workers' union and the AtlantiCare Medical Center. Both are self-insured—they are large enough to pay for their workers' health care directly, and both have been hammered by the exploding costs. As for the union, its contracts are frequently for workers' total compensation—wages plus benefits. It gets a fixed pot. Year after year, the low-wage busboys, hotel cleaners, and kitchen staff have voted against sacrificing their health benefits. As a result, they have gone without a wage increase for years. Out of desperation, the union's health fund and the hospital decided to try something new. The hospital provided the floor space.

The Special Care Center reinvented the idea of a primary-care clinic in almost every way. The union and the hospital (financial departments) agreed to switch from paying the doctors for every individual office visit and treatment; instead, they started paying a flat monthly fee for each patient. That cut the huge expense that most clinics incur from billing paperwork. The patients were given unlimited access to the clinic without charges—no co-payments, no insurance bills. Fernandopulle, the director of The Special Care Center, explained that this would force doctors on staff to focus on service, in order to retain their patients and the fees they would bring.

The new payment paradigm also allowed Fernandopulle to design the clinic around the things that sick, expensive patients most need and value, rather than the ones that pay the best. He adopted an open-access scheduling system to guarantee same-day appointments for the acutely ill. He customized an electronic information system that tracks whether patients are meeting their goals. And, he staffed the clinic with people who would help them do it.

The clinic holds a staff meeting each morning to review the medical issues of the patients on the appointment books. One of their keys to success was there Health Coaches. Each health coach works with patients—in person, by phone, by e-mail—to help them manage their health. The coaches work with the doctors, but see their patients far more frequently than the doctors do, at least once every two weeks. Their most important attribute, Fernandopulle explained, is a knack for connecting with sick people, and understanding their difficulties. Most of the coaches come from their patients' communities and speak their languages. Many have experience with chronic illness in their own families. (One was himself a patient in the clinic). Few had clinical experience. One worked the register at a Dunkin' Donuts. Another was a Sears retail manager. A third was an administrative assistant at a casino. "We recruit for attitude and train for skill," the clinic had said, when discussing their philosophy.

In doing my research, I had the opportunity to speak with a lot of people. They had a wide range of stories and perspectives. I have come to the conclusion that the Affordable Healthcare Act has many good points. It is also very much a hot button issue and very partisan.

The Black perspective is that affordable healthcare is a good thing. Any candidate courting the Black vote has to be able to articulate the need, to tweak it, while extolling the virtues in a way they, the candidate, can actually live with. The cost savings from flat rate coverage A.C.O.'s and Medicaid A.C.O.'s are certainly real. We need to create a legislation mandating where those savings go, like a split between doctors, who come on board, preventative care, and on the Medicaid side, moving some of the existing personnel into the role of life coaches in areas where A.C.O. have not yet been set up. Candidates that want our support need to bring down the cost without cutting people off from valuable Healthcare; this will give the candidates the support they are looking for. As a people, we have more chronic illness than most. We need affordable healthcare.

Chapter 13

Financial Empowerment and Job Creation

We need Welfare Reform. The current welfare system incentivizes men and women not to be married. In the welfare system, as it is now, women get more support if the father is not around. They are forced to give information on the father, so he can be forced to pay child support. In a lot of cases, that couple is still a couple, and they are trying to see if they can work it out and stay together. That needs to be the other way around. That family needs to get incentives for staying together.

When a couple has a child and stays together that family has a better chance for long term success. That child has the benefit of both parents in the home. They say children learn more from their parents in their first few years on behavior, manners, and morals. They learn their code of conduct at home. With 2 parents in the home, the child has a better chance of becoming a better adjusted member of society. Which costs the taxpayers more, the family stays together, are assigned a life coach, and a stipend to bring them up to the living wage level.

Let's run the numbers. If a couple is together on welfare and has 2 children, and each works for $8/hr, under this new reform, they would get the following:

1. A life coach		$500(an)
2. Living wage stipend to $14/hr (an)		$23,040
3. Food stamps		$1,320(an)
4. Section 8 voucher		<u>$6,000(an)</u>
		$30,860(an)

Couple not together (family of 3)

1	Life coach (2)	$ 500(an)
2	T.A.N.F.	$5,088(an)
3	Food stamps	$4,200(an)
4	Section 8 voucher	$16,200(an)
5	Medicaid	
		<u>$14,043(an)</u>
		$40,031(an)

As you can see, there is an immediate savings under this reform. You can further incentivize the family by giving them a $1,000 bonus at the end of every year they stay gainfully employed as a requirement of the program. The bonus would be payable at the end of five years in a lump sum. Also, as they remain employed, their wages will go up and taxpayer will save even more.

With this kind of reform, the effect of the new Health and Human Services Directive, in regards to employment waivers for the States, will be minimized (see appendix). Subsequently, 112TH CONGRESS, 2D SESSION, H. R. 6140 (see appendix) should be amended to include appropriate reform, and not just knee jerk reform.

People will see a way out through this new form of welfare. Work ethics will improve. Families will stay together. You will see less people turning to crime as a way of living. You will see a drop in the divorce rate and an increase in the marriage rate. You will start to see an increase in the strength of families in our communities, and our communities themselves will be stronger.

A reform like this will enable Black men to come back home and feel good. It will help to give them their self-respect back. For the first time in this nation's history, you would be enacting a reform that would give Blacks a hand up, not a hand-out. This reform would go a long way towards empowering the Black community.

An empowered community will fight to defend those that have empowered them.

If the provisions of the Affordable Healthcare Reform Acts A.C.O.'s are also allowed to stand, across the country, we are looking at over 500,000 jobs created. At least 100,000 of them, will be the life coach position. These can be filled by well screened current welfare recipients. This will further lower the welfare program rolls and costs.

With the living wage stipend in place, you will see people willing to take jobs they never would have before. If you know the only job you can find is a cashier job at a corner store. It won't matter because you're going to be motivated to keep that job to continue to get that living wage stipend and be able to take care of your family.

This welfare reform will also help small business owners and budding entrepreneurs. This reform would give small business owners the opportunity to hire new employees from a new untapped pool. This would allow business to grow. Our economy is driven by small business and entrepreneurs. To enact welfare reform in this manner would allow the business sector to feed the economy the way it was intended. Growing businesses means a growing economy.

White Folks Guide to Understanding the Black Community

The long term economic and psychological advantages for the economy, and the country as a whole, far outweigh any economic concerns. The benefit of strengthening families has exponential value for beyond dollars and cents. Families are the cornerstones of our communities. Welfare reform is necessary to build <u>strong</u> families, which leads to strong communities.

The next step in true self sustainability is understanding money. We all know what money is, but few of us really understand money, especially, what it means and what it does. We want to include a mandatory financial literacy component. We want to teach the importance of good credit, how to plan for financial future, retirement, rainy days, and education. This will cost you nothing.

Service providers will be clamoring to get at a new market. Those that are interested in providing the financial literacy component need to be properly vetted. They need to be able to deal with a challenging clientele, meaning they need to be prepared to start from scratch. The program needs to start as far back, and basic, as how to balance a checkbook.

Intermediate financial literacy should include an economic perspective. People need to understand what drives our economy. People need to understand what role they play in our national economy, and how they can benefit themselves and our economy as a whole. People also need to understand national spending, the deficit, and the role taxes play.

Advanced financial literacy should cover and introduce to the people the global economy and marketplace. People need to understand what "Buy American" means and how it works in our economy. People need to have a basic understanding of global financial markets. They need to know what they are and what they do. They need to understand how all this impacts not only our economy, but especially prices at home.

Welfare reform, as it is outlined here, is necessary, but it is not enough. Financial literacy is a must. Only with both components in place do we properly address the phrase, "Give a man a fish, feed him for a day, but teach him how to fish, and you feed him for a lifetime". It's fishing season and class needs to be in session.

Chapter 14

Tax Reform, Moderated Flat Tax,

Limited deductions for individuals that give to Abbot and Title 1 schools; Business credit given to businesses that support Healthcare Reform and hire welfare recipients

In this country, we have been in need of serious tax reform for some time. People that pay taxes complain they pay too much. Because of this, many politicians campaign against having new taxes, or tax reduction. Most don't deliver.

People want to control where their tax dollars are going. They want more say in government spending. Better yet, they would love to curtail government spending. The government claims it needs to raise taxes, so it can spend more on things that we still can't agree on. Since taxation was written into the constitution, and it is the logical way to fund government, we can't exactly get rid of taxes all together.

Currently, the United States Tax Revenue Code is over 9 million words long and has a lot of loop holes. Many of these loopholes, deductions, and exemptions make collecting taxes and enforcing tax laws more complicated than they need to be. The current tax law slows economic growth with all of its convoluted economic incentives. Many of the codes clauses allow and even encourage, tax avoidance. This of course only applies to those that understand tax law.

As Blacks, we pay taxes for the most part with little regard to where they go and what they are used for. We complain the government takes too much from the little people and not enough from the rich. When we hear tax cuts, we pay little attention because the perception is tax cuts only help the rich. When we hear tax increases, we assume it will hurt us. Many times it does.

According to *Investopedia a website dedicated to all things financial,* the definition of 'Flat Tax' is a system that applies the same tax rate to every taxpayer regardless of income bracket. A flat tax applies the same tax rate to all taxpayers, with no deductions or exemptions allowed. Supporters of a flat tax system propose that it would give taxpayers incentive to earn more because they would not be penalized with a higher tax bracket. In addition, supporters argue that a flat tax system is fairer because it imposed the tax on all taxpayers regardless of income. In a marginal progressive tax system, which we have now, individuals who make more money are taxed at a higher rate. Many of the countries that have imposed a flat tax rate system on individuals and businesses, including Estonia, Lithuania and Latvia, have experienced economic growth, since they adopted flat tax rate policies.

With a flat tax, or a moderated flat tax, there are fewer reasons to create tax shelters and other forms of tax evasion. A Flat tax is not new. Over the years, it has been proposed as a way to simplify the tax code. The current progressive, or graduated marginal tax code, is over 72,000 pages as of 2009. Less than a quarter of one of those pages would be needed with a moderated flat tax code. This would simplify tax code and taxes, making taxes fair for all.

A Flat tax with limited deductions, or moderated flat taxes, would allow for few deductions and close many loop holes. It would still allow for charitable deductions and home mortgage interests, which are the most discussed exceptions. These are popular with voters and often used. Another theme is a single, large, fixed deduction; the idea is that a blanket deduction rolls up a whole host of fixed living costs. I would include in this deductions for education, healthcare, and welfare reform, which is also outlined here.

For education, there should be an additional credit for those who opt to have their tax dollars go to a Title 1 or Abott school. Many people complain about their tax dollars funding failing schools. It should include an incentive to support schools in need. They should have a stake in the progress of the schools the same way a stock holder has a stake in business. The districts would know if they want to keep their funding they have to actually educate our children well.

The cost savings from flat rate coverage A.C.O.'s and Medicaid A.C.O.'s, under the current healthcare reform, are real. A portion of those savings should be given to the doctors who join the A.C.O.'s in the form of incentive tax credits. This would encourage doctors to work with the tax payer cost saving A.C.O.'s. This would also in turn provide better, and more personal care, for our more chronically ill and costly patients.

For business owners, there should be a credit incentive to hire welfare recipients. Under the proposed welfare reform, current welfare recipients will receive a living wage subsidy to supplement their earned wage from employment. Those that hire the welfare recipients should get a tax credit. This would also help business owners offset the cost of healthcare for these new hires under the new healthcare reform.

With a flat tax system another positive effect would be to discourage increased government spending. The reason for this is that any tax increase would affect all taxpayers. In the current tax system, government officials are able to win the approval of the public by raising taxes on certain groups to pay for new spending. If everyone's taxes go up with any new spending, every new government program would be more carefully scrutinized. In the long run, this would be cause government to become more efficient.

With a flat tax, all income could be taxed once at its source. Hall and Rabushka (1995) proposed an amendment to the U.S. Revenue Code with a type of variation of the flat tax they liked. This amendment was only a few pages long. It would have replaced hundreds of pages. As it now stands, the U.S. Revenue Code is over 9 million words long. It has a lot of loopholes, deductions, and exemptions, which make the collection of taxes and the enforcement of tax law complicated and inefficient.

Under a moderated flat tax companies could simply, every period, make a single payment to the government covering the flat tax liabilities of their employees and the taxes owed on their business income. For example, suppose that in a given year, ACME earns a profit of 3 million, pays 2 million in salaries, and spends an added 1 million on other expenses the IRS deems to be taxable income, such as stock options, bonuses, and certain executive privileges. Given a flat rate of 15%, ACME would then owe the IRS (3M + 2M + 1M) × 0.15 = 900,000. This payment would, in one fell swoop, settle the tax liabilities of ACME's employees as well as taxes it owed by being a firm. Most employees throughout the economy would never need to interact with the IRS, as all tax owed on wages, interest, dividends, royalties, etc. would be withheld at the source. The main exceptions would be employees with incomes from personal ventures.

For those that opt to take advantage of the few remaining deductions, the process would be a little different. They would file a return based on their deductions and get a refund. For some this would be the first time in a long time, if ever, that they would be eligible for a refund. Some claim that such a system would reduce the number of entities required to file returns from about 130 million individuals, households, and businesses, as at present, to a mere 8 million businesses and self-employed.

Pastor Shannon Wright

Part VI

How to Get Out the Vote

Actions Speak Louder than Words, so
Talk Soft and Carry a Big Stick.

Chapter 15

Read the book. Know who we are, and understand what we need and say it in a way that sounds like what we want to hear.

We, as Blacks, have not yet reached actual real equality in the area of voting rights. We make up 14% of the population as a whole; and, we also make up about 1/3 of those who are ineligible to vote because of criminal convictions. I am sure there are those some even reading this book that would say our incarceration rate is higher because more of us are criminals. I suppose that is a matter of perception, although it saddens me to know there are those that think of us that way. With the ever accruing legislative changes to the implementation of our rights and abilities to vote, I am sure this issue will continue to evolve (and hopefully the change will be for the better). We will need both our legal minds and moral conscience to find where we belong on this issue.

One thing I can tell you is this: Please, do not just come to our Churches, community centers, senior centers, and schools, like clockwork, just in time for election days. It is transparent and insulting. Politics should be about the people. It should not be about some of the people, in some of the places, some of the time. Politics is about all of the people—all of the time. If it is not your intention to represent your whole district, then please don't bother to attempt to placate us with a photo op tour through the hood.

If you want us to vote, don't just speak at us. Craft a message that speaks to us. Meet us, where we are. Don't stand on the mountain top. Tell us what you think we need. Lend a hand, so we can get to the mountain top with you. Then, set a table, and invite us to break bread at your table. You will have our full attention.

Chapter 16

It's Not What You Say, but How You Say It, the blitz

Usually the blitz would be phase 2 of your "get out the vote" effort. It would usually start a few days before Election Day. That logic does not work for the Black community, unless you are a rock star candidate. We don't trust you, and we don't believe you. This is partly because of being dulled down and dumbed down through the process and evolution of the entitlement mentality.

We are accustomed to candidates running through our neighborhoods a few weeks before an election. The problem is we know we won't see you again, until the next election. We know you don' put much stock in our votes. So, we don't put much stock in you.

If you want to get our attention, come to us first. Let us know we really matter to you. Make us feel like our issues are of concern to you.

Start your blitz early. Get us involved. Include us in the planning and development phase of your campaign, not just the photo ops. Know our issues.

Identify those people that have similar mind sets to yours. Ask them questions, and then <u>listen</u> to what they tell you and incorporate it in your overall strategy. Then, publically give them credit for it. Show yourself an involved team player.

If you start your blitz early enough, you could go into our neighborhoods, identify supporters, and make them neighborhood captains. Their whole job would be to go to the folks they know in the neighborhood that also want something different, and motivate them to get involved.

Have competitions and give prizes. Have a t-shirt design contest, have a team spirit contest, or a recruitment contest. Whichever one you choose is obviously up to you. The bottom line is that you want to reach out as early as you can, and make sure to be sincere and inclusive.

If you want us to not just believe you, but to also believe <u>in you</u>, you need to make us more than an afterthought. Come in to our neighborhoods early and blitz early.

Chapter 17

You Catch More Flies with Honey than Vinegar

If the goal of your, Get-Out the Vote, campaign is to identify who your supporters are, and get as many of them as possible to actually go vote for you, you are going about it all the wrong way, especially if you want to attract the Black vote. Your GOTV team is not responsible for persuading people to support your candidate. That job belongs to the rest of your campaign structure. The GOVT team's job, and their only job, is to get people to the poles to vote. However, it is your job to get them the necessary tools they need to effectively get their job done.

No one needs to tell us that it is our civic responsibility to vote. We do not need perks or rewards other than knowing we have exercised our right to vote; we have played our part in the shaping of the future. Yet, for many, that may not be enough.

Those that would be inclined to vote, yet still do not vote with any regularity, fall into 2 main categories. In the first category are those whose schedule just doesn't allow them to get to the polls on Election Day. I know you are probably thinking that is what absentee ballots are for, and that is very true. However, the problem is these voters often already feel like their vote won't really matter anyway. In the second category are those that meant to vote, but there were higher priorities on their lists that day, so they did not actually go out and vote.

For the first group, the ones that just don't have time, plan out a, Get-Out the Vote Absentee Ballot, campaign. Also, do a series of public service announcements with celebrity spokespeople; or at least, get local known personalities to urge people to get their absentee ballot in. The second group just needs to be engaged and excited about Election Day and voting. Both of these groups need an Election Day motivator to get the numbers up.

The Get-Out the Vote campaign usually only needs to do two things in order to encourage voters. The first job is to identify who is already a committed supporter of the candidate. Their second job is to get those supporters to go out and vote. This GOTV effort normally would set a goal to secure at least 10% of the voters you need to win the election. In most cases, that would be considered a success and successful plan.

White Folks Guide to Understanding the Black Community

If your victory on Election Day is predicated on, or includes, getting out the vote from the Black community (or any other hard to reach community or group) that 10%, which is the norm, will not be enough to ensure victory. Your target needs to be 25% - 35% of that voting block. We are a hard to predict people. You need to build in a cushion.

Some may have a problem with this, but truth is truth. If you want to insure enough votes, if you want us to come out and vote, you have to do something for us. Show us you are investing in us. We are a you first and us maybe people. It can even be an event for the community. You can't just come to town and get us to vote for you. Again, unless you are a rock star, plan to spend money in our communities and not on your campaign in our communities. In fact, spend money in our communities.

Chapter 18

Let Yea without Sin Cast the First Stone

In the last few chapters, I have outlined a modified GOTV effort targeted towards the Black community, which incidentally can be modified for use in any hard to reach population. "When I was a child, I talked like a child, I thought like a child, I reasoned like a child. When I became a man [or woman], I put childish ways behind me." *1 Cor. 13:11*

You must understand many of us still need to grow up. I myself had my epiphany a few years ago out of the mouths of babes. My son asked me a question that said a whole lot! As Blacks we are Democrats. As adults, we need to evaluate who we are, and what we stand for as individuals and not based on hearsay. There comes a time when you define yourself. It's called growing up, and for some of us it takes longer than for others.

Let me give you a historical perspective on why we are where we are politically. When the Civil War, ended our struggle for equality began. Most blacks saw

White Folks Guide to Understanding the Black Community

the Republican Party as the party of freedom. During Reconstruction, this was true. After Reconstruction, the Republican Party became a minority party in the South with very few white Republicans. The Democrats, or the three "s" party: slavery, secession and segregation, had all the power.

Blacks in the South were left to fight for themselves. The Republican Party left them to build alliances of their own. This didn't work. The last thing the racist South wanted were free blacks, they wanted free labor and power. The violence in the South against the freedmen was unbearable. Many injustices were committed at the hands of racist Democrats. When the Republicans tried to help, they were stopped by the majority, which were the Democrats.

President Theodore Roosevelt tried to intervene. He could not stop the incidents of involuntary servitude. Blacks felt abandoned and left the party in droves, especially when the Democrats started offering social programs to take care of "the little man."

Republicans kept offering a hand up and Democrats a handout. Handouts were easier they were accepted over a hand up. Even folks that did not take handouts, they were glad that they were there, so somebody else would be responsible for our brothers and sisters in the community.

Pastor Shannon Wright

We voted to keep government handouts going. This became a syndrome; it affected everyone. We didn't know the literal and figurative cost. Back then, we weren't taught those things. Today, we still aren't at least not in a way we can relate to. The entitlement mentality has crippled us. Many of us now actually believe it is government's responsibility to take care of us.

All of this being said, don't judge us. Don't lecture us, don't talk down to us, don't overlook us or take us for granted. Meet us where we are and set a place for us at the table. Judge not least ye be judged and ye without sin cast the first stone.

<u>Summary</u>

We are a people of dreams, hopes and desires. We are full of promise. We are the untapped resource. In writing this book, I logged a lot of hours of research. I learned things. I grew as a person. For me, there is no turning back. Am I My Brother's Keeper? Yes, Yes I Am.

Let this book serve as a clarion call to all those who believe and know the time is now to make a move, the time is now to take a stand. To all the preachers, who turn a blind eye to the suffering in their communities and preach for 2 hours on their prosperity ministry with no regard for the true meaning of their calling, I'm coming for you. To all the educators, who spend our tax dollars with an unspoken commitment to educate our children who are our future, collect their paychecks and happily turn our children into the streets with the intellectual ability of a fly, I'm coming for you. Lastly, to all the so called politicians and community leaders, who continue to lead us like blind animals to slaughter, as they line their pockets and bank accounts, I'm coming for you.

The preachers, teachers, and politicians are the perfect trifecta to either our salvation or our demise. We all look to you to lead us and to teach us. Under your guidance we will prosper or perish. You shape the future. Your deeds will no longer be allowed to plague and fester in our communities. To those much is given, much is also expected. We will stand by faith on that mountain of expectations, knowing that faith without works is dead. It's time to get to work!

Appendix

1. The New Deal Program

The main New Deal programs were Agricultural Adjustment Act. They protected farmers from price drops by providing crop subsidies to reduce production, and educational programs to teach methods of preventing soil erosion. The Civil Works Administration provided public works jobs at $15/week to four million workers in 1934, ended in 1934 in large part due to opposition to its cost. The Federal Emergency Relief Act distributed millions of dollars of direct aid to unemployed workers. The Glass-Steagall Act (FDIC, 1933) created federally insured bank deposits ($2500 per investor at first) to prevent bank failures. National Industrial Recovery Act (NIRA, 1933) created NRA to enforce codes of fair competition, minimum wages, and to permit collective bargaining of workers was declared unconstitutional in the landmark Supreme Court case (*Schechter Poultry Corp. v. US.*). The Supreme Court ruled that the NRA violated the separation of powers. The National Youth Administration (NYA, 1935) provided part-time employment to more than two million college and high school students. Also, the Public Works Administration (PWA, 1933) received $3.3 billion appropriation from Congress for public works projects (It ended in 1941). The Rural Electrification Administration (REA, 1935) encouraged farmers to join cooperatives to bring electricity to farms. Despite its efforts, by 1940 only 40% of American farms were electrified. Securities and Exchange Commission (SEC, 1934) regulated stock market and restricted margin buying. Social Security Act (SSA, 1935) response to critics (Dr. Townsend and Huey Long), it provided pensions, unemployment insurance, and aid to blind, deaf, disabled, and dependent children. The Tennessee Valley Authority (TVA, 1933), Federal government build series of dams to prevent flooding and sell electricity (the first public competition with private power industries). The Wagner Act (NLRB, 1935), allowed workers to join unions and outlawed union-busting tactics by management), and Works Progress Administration (WPA, 1935, Employed 8.5 million workers in construction and other jobs, but more importantly provided work in arts, theater, and literary projects, officially ended in 1943)

2. Below is an essay written by a teacher in reference to his experiences teaching Black students:

What Is It Like to Teach Black Students?

by Christopher Jackson

Until recently, I taught at a predominantly black high school in a southeastern state. The mainstream press only gives a hint of what the conditions are like in black schools, and only a hint. The expressions that journalists use such as, "chaotic" or "poor learning environments" or "lack of discipline" do not capture what really happens in those schools. There is nothing like the day-to-day experience of teaching Black children and that story is what I will try to convey.

One of the most immediately striking things about my students was that so many of them were loud. They had little conception of ordinary decorum. It was not unusual for five students to be screaming at me at once. It did no good to try to quiet them, and white women were particularly inept at trying. Once, I sat in on one woman's class as she begged the children to pipe down. They just yelled louder so their voices would be heard over hers. Many of the students seemed to have no conception of waiting for an appropriate time to say something.

The students would get ideas in their heads and simply would have to shout them out. For instance, I lead a discussion on government, and suddenly, I was interrupted by a student who said, "We gotta get more Democrats! Clinton, she good!" The student seemed to be content with that outburst, but two minutes later, he would suddenly start yelling again: "Clinton good!"

It was not uncommon for 15 boys to swagger into a classroom, bouncing their shoulders and jiving back. They were yelling back and forth, rapping 15 different sets of words in the same harsh, rasping dialect. The words were almost invariably a childish form of boasting:.

"Who got dem shine rim, who got dem shine shoe, who got dem shine grill (gold and silver dental caps)?"

The amateur rapper would often then end with a claim—in the crudest terms imaginable:

"All womankind is sexually devoted to me".

For whatever reason, many of my students would often groan instead of saying a particular word, as in, "She suck dat aaahhhh (think of a long grinding groan), she f**k dat aaaahhhh, she lick dat aaaahhh."

So many black girls dance in the hall, in the classroom, on the chairs, next to the chairs, under the chairs, everywhere. Once I had to take a call on my cell phone and stepped outside of class. I was away about two minutes, but when I got back, girls had lined up at the front of the classroom and were convulsing to the delight of the boys.

Blacks, overall, are the most directly critical people I have ever met,

"Dat shirt stupid,"or " Yo' kid a bastard," or " Yo' lips big."

Unlike whites, who tread gingerly around the subject of race, Blacks can be brutally to the point.

Once, I needed to send a student to the office to deliver a message. I asked for volunteers, and suddenly you would think my classroom was a bastion of civic engagement. Thirty hands shot into the air. I picked a light-skinned boy to deliver the message. One very dark student was indignant,

"You pick da half-breed," He said.

And immediately other Blacks cried out, screaming, "He half-breed!"

For decades, the country has been lamenting the poor academic performance of Blacks and there is much to lament. There is no question that many Blacks come to school with a serious handicap that is not their fault. At home, they learn a dialect that is almost a different language. They not only mispronounce words, but their grammar is often wrong.

When a Black wants to ask, "Where is the bathroom?" he may actually say, "Whar da badroom be?" Grammatically, this is the equivalent of "Where the bathroom is?" And this is the way they speak in high school. Students write the way they speak, so this is the language that shows up in written assignments.

It is true that some whites face a similar handicap. They speak with what I would call "a country" accent that is hard to reproduce, but results in sentences such as, "I'm gonna gemme a Coke." Some of these country whites had to learn correct pronunciation and usage. The difference is that most whites overcome this handicap and learn to speak correctly; many Blacks do not.

Most of the Blacks I taught simply had no interest in academic subjects. I taught history, and students would often say they didn't want to do an assignment or they didn't like history because it was all about white people. Of course, this was "diversity" history, in which every cowboy's Black cook got a special page on how he contributed to winning the West, but Black children still found it inadequate.

So, I would throw up my hands and assign them a project on a real, historical, black person. My favorite was Marcus Garvey. They had never heard of him, and I would tell them to research him, but most of them never did. They didn't care, and they didn't want to do any work.

Anyone who teaches Blacks soon learns that they have a completely different view of government from whites. Once, I decided to have students write about one thing the government should do to improve America. I gave this question to three classes totaling about 100 students, approximately 80 of whom were Black.

My white students came back with generally conservative ideas. Such as, "We need to cut off people who don't work", and this was the most common suggestion.

Nearly every Black gave a variation on the theme of, "We need more government services."

143

My students had only the vaguest notion of who pays for government services. For them, it was like a magical piggy bank that never went empty.

One Black girl was exhorting the class on the need for more social services, and I kept trying to explain that people, real live people, are taxed for the money to pay for those services.

"Yeah, it come from whites," she finally said, and then added, "They stingy anyway."

"Many Black people make over $50,000 dollars a year and you would also be taking away from your own people," I said.

She had an answer to that, "Dey half breed."

The class agreed. I let the subject drop.

Many Black girls are perfectly happy to be welfare queens. On career day, one girl explained to the class that she was going to have lots of children and get fat checks from the government. No one in the class seemed to have any objection to this career choice.

Surprising attitudes of the students can come out in class discussions. Once, we were talking about the crimes committed in the aftermath of Hurricane Katrina, and I brought up the rape of a young girl in the bathroom of the

Superdome. A majority of my students believed this was a horrible crime, but a few took it lightly.

One Black boy spoke up without raising his hand, "Dat no big deal. They thought they is gonna die, so they figured they have some fun. Dey jus' wanna have a fun time. You know what I'm sayin'?" A few Black heads nodded in agreement.

My department head once asked all the teachers to get a response from all the students to the following question, "Do you think it is okay to break the law if it
will benefit you greatly?"

By then, I had been teaching for a while and was not surprised by answers that left a young, liberal, white woman colleague aghast.

"Yeah", was the favorite answer.

One student explained, "Get dat green."

How the world looks to Blacks (still from the essay written by Christopher Jackson)

One point on which most Blacks agree is that everything is "racis'." This is one message of liberalism they have absorbed completely.

Did you do your homework? "Na, homework racis'."

Why did you get an F on the test? "Test racis'."

I was trying to teach a unit on British philosophers, discussing Bentham, Hobbes, and Locke, and the first thing I heard from the students was, "Dey all white! Where da black philosophers'?"

I tried to explain there were no Blacks in eighteenth century Britain. You can probably guess what they said to that, "Dat racis'!"

One student accused me of deliberately failing him on a test because I didn't like Black people.

"Do you think I really hate Black people?"

"Yeah."

"Have I done anything to make you feel this way? How do you know?"

"You just do."

"Why do you say that?"

He just smirked, looked out the window, and sucked air through his teeth.

Perhaps this was a regional thing, but the Blacks often sucked air through their teeth, as a wordless expression of disdain or hostility.

My students were sometimes unable to see the world except through the lens of their own blackness. I had a class that was host to a German exchange student. One day he put on a Power Point presentation with famous German landmarks as well as his school and family. From time to time during the presentation, Blacks would scream, "Where da Black folk?!" The exasperated German tried to explain that there were no black people where he lived in Germany. The students did not believe him. I told them Germany is in Europe, where white people are from, and Africa is where Black people are from. They insisted that the German student was racist and deliberately refused to associate with Blacks.

Blacks are keenly interested in their own racial characteristics. I have learned, for example, that some blacks have "good hair." Good hair is black parlance for black-white hybrid hair. Apparently, it is less kinky, easier to style, and considered more attractive.

Blacks are also proud of light skin. Imagine two black students shouting insults across the room. One is dark and slim, the other light and obese. The dark one begins the exchange, "You fat, Ridario!" And, Ridario smiles, doesn't deign to look at his detractor, and shakes his head like a wobbling top, saying, "You wish you light skinned." They could go on like this, repeating the same insults over and over.

My Black students had nothing. but contempt for Hispanic immigrants. They would vent their feelings so crudely that our department strongly advised us never to talk about immigration in class in case the principal or some outsider might overhear. Whites were "racis'," of course, but they thought of us at least as Americans, but not the Mexicans.

Blacks have a certain understanding of white people, not necessarily hostile. They know how whites act, and it is clear they believe whites are smart and are good at organizing things. At the same time, they probably suspect whites are just putting on an act when they talk about equality, as if it is all a sham that makes it easier for whites to control Blacks. Blacks want a bigger piece of the American pie. I'm convinced that if it were up to them they would give whites a considerably smaller piece than whites get now, but they would give them something. They wouldn't give Mexicans anything.

What about Black boys and white girls? No one is supposed to notice this or talk about it, but it is glaringly obvious: Black boys are obsessed with white girls. I've witnessed the following drama countless times. A Black boy saunters up to a white girl. The cocky black dances around her, not really in a menacing way. It's more a shuffle than a threat. As he bobs and shuffles he asks, "When you gonna go wit' me?" There are two kinds of reply. The more confident white girl gets annoyed, looks away from the Black and shouts, "I don't wanna go out with you!" The more demure girl will look at her feet and mumble a polite excuse, but ultimately say no. There is only one response from the Black boy: "You racis'." Many girls—all too many—actually feel guilty because they do not want to date Blacks. Most white girls at my school stayed away from Blacks, but a few, particularly the ones who were addicted to drugs, fell in with them.

There is something else that is striking about Blacks. So many Black people that I have observed, seem to have no sense of romance or of falling in love. What brings men and women together is sex, pure and simple, and there is a crude openness about this. There were many degenerate whites, of course, but some of my white students were capable of real devotion and tenderness, emotions that seemed absent from most Blacks—especially the boys.

Black schools are violent and the few whites who are too poor to escape are caught in the storm. The violence is astonishing, not so much that it happens, but the atmosphere in which it happens. Blacks can be smiling, seemingly perfectly content with what they are doing, having a good time, and then, suddenly start fighting. It's uncanny. Not long ago, I was walking through the halls, and a group of Black boys were walking in front of me. All of a sudden, they started fighting with another group in the hallway.

Blacks are extraordinarily quick to take offense. Once, I accidentally scuffed a Black boy's white sneaker with my shoe. He immediately rubbed his body up against mine and threatened to attack me. I stepped outside the class and had a security guard escort the student to the office. It was unusual for students to threaten teachers physically this way, but among themselves, they were quick to fight for similar reasons.

The real victims are the unfortunate whites caught in this. They are always in danger and their educations suffer. White weaklings are particularly susceptible, but mostly to petty violence. They may be slapped or get a couple of kicks when they are trying to open a bottom locker. Typically, Blacks save the hard,serious violence for each other.

There was a lot of promiscuous sex among my students and this led to violence. Black girls were constantly fighting over Black boys. It was not uncommon to see two girls literally ripping each other's hair out with a police officer in the middle trying to break up the fight. The Black boy they were fighting over would be standing by with a smile, enjoying the show he had created. For reasons I cannot explain, boys seldom fought over girls.

Pregnancy was common among the Blacks, though many Black girls were so fat, I could not tell the difference. I don't know how many girls got abortions, but when they have the baby, they usually stayed in school, and had their own parents look after the child. The school did not offer daycare.

Aside from the police officers constantly on campus, security guards were everywhere in Black schools—we had one in every hall. They also sat in on unruly classes and escorted students to the office. They were unarmed, but worked closely with the three city police officers who were constantly on duty.

There was a lot of drug dealing at my school. This was a way to make a fair amount of money, but it also gave boys power over girls who wanted drugs. An addicted girl—Black or white—became the plaything of anyone who could get her drugs.

One of my students was a notorious drug dealer. Everyone knew it. He was 19 years old and in eleventh grade. Once, he got a score of three out of 100 on a test. He had been locked up four times since he was 13.

One day, I asked him, "Why do you come to school?"

He wouldn't answer. He just looked out the window, smiled, and sucked air through his teeth.

His friend Yidarius ventured an explanation, "He get dat green and get dem females." "

"What is the green?" I asked. "Money or dope?"

"Both," said Yidarius with a smile.

A very fat student interrupted from across the room, "We get dat lunch, Mr. Jackson, we gotta get dat lunch and brickfuss."

What he meant was the free breakfast and lunch poor students got every day.

Another shouted back, "Nigga, we know'd you be lovin' brickfuss!"

Some readers may believe that I have drawn a cruel caricature of Black students. They go from grade to grade, practically pushed through, but they finally get their diplomas because there is so much pressure on teachers to get them through. It saves money to move them along, the school looks good, and the teachers look good. Many of these children should fail, but the system would then crack under their weight if they were all held back.

How did my experience make me feel about Blacks? Ultimately, I lost sympathy for them. In so many ways, they seem to make their own beds. There they are in an integrationist's fantasy—in the same classroom with white students, eating the same lunch, using the same bathrooms, listening to the same teachers—and yet the Blacks fail while the whites pass.

There is an unutterable secret among teachers. Almost all teachers realize that Blacks do not respond to traditional white instruction. Does that put the lie to environmentalism? Not at all; it is what brings about endless, pointless innovation that is supposed to bring Blacks up to the white level. For example, teachers are told that Blacks need hands-on instruction and more group work. Teachers are told that Blacks are more vocal and do not learn through reading and lectures. The implication is that they have certain traits that lend themselves to a different kind of teaching.

Whites have learned a certain way for centuries, but it just doesn't work with Blacks. Of course, this implies racial differences, but if pressed, most liberal teachers would say different racial learning styles come from some indefinable cultural characteristic unique to Blacks. Therefore, schools must change, America must change; but, into what? How do you turn quantum physics into hands-on instruction or group work? No one knows, but we must keep changing until we find something that works. Public school has certainly changed since anyone reading this was a student.

Blacks break down the intimacy that can be achieved in the classroom, and leave you convinced that that intimacy is really a form of kinship. Just last year, I read on the bathroom stall the words "F**k Whitey." Not two feet away, on the same stall, was a small swastika

It is impossible to get them to care about such abstractions as property rights or democratic citizenship. They do not see much further than the fact that you live in a big house and "we in da pro-jek." Of course, there are a few loutish whites who will never think past their next meal and a few sensitive Blacks for whom anything is possible, but no society takes on the characteristics of its exceptions.

Once, I asked my students, "What do you think of the Constitution?"

"It white," one slouching Black rang out.

The class began to laugh. And, I caught myself laughing along with them. I was laughing while Pompeii's volcano simmers, while the barbarians swell around the Palatine, while the country I love, and the job I love, and the community I love become dimmer by the day.

At some level, my students understood the same thing as I did. One day, I asked the bored, Black faces,staring back at me, "What would happen if all the white people in America disappeared tomorrow?"

"We screwed," a young, pitch-black boy screamed back. The rest of the blacks laughed.

I have had children tell me to my face, as they struggled with an assignment, "I cain't do dis, Mr. Jackson,I black."

The point is that human beings are not always rational. Most whites do not think Black Americans could ever do anything so irrational. They see Blacks on television smiling, fighting evil whites, embodying white values. But, the real Black is not on television, and you pull your purse closer when you see him, and you lock the car doors when he swaggers by with his pants hanging down almost to his knees.

3.Temporary Assistance for Needy Families

U.S. Department of Health and Human Services
Administration for Children and Families
Office of Family Assistance
Washington, D.C. 20447

Information Memorandum

Transmittal No. TANF-ACF-IM-2012-03	Date: July 12, 2012

TO: States administering the Temporary Assistance for Needy Families (TANF) Program and other interested parties

SUBJECT: Guidance concerning waiver and expenditure authority under Section 1115

REFERENCE: Section 1115 of the Social Security Act. [42 U.S.C. 1315]; Section 402 of the Social Security Act. [42 U.S.C. 602]

BACKGROUND: Section 1115 of the Social Security Act provides authority for the Secretary of the Department of Health and Human Services (HHS) to consider and approve experimental, pilot, or demonstration projects which, in the Secretary's judgment, are likely to assist in promoting the objectives of Title IV-A. Section 1115 allows for waiver of compliance with section 402 of the Social Security Act to the extent and for the period necessary to enable a state to carry out an approved project. The statute also provides authority for costs of such projects which would not otherwise be an allowable use of funds under Part A of Title IV to be regarded as an allowable use of funds, to the extent and for the period approved.

As specified in statute, the purpose of Part A is to increase the flexibility of states in operating a program designed to: (1) provide assistance to needy families so that children may be cared for in their own homes or in the homes of relatives; (2) end the dependence of needy parents on government benefits by promoting job preparation, work, and marriage; (3) prevent and reduce the incidence of out-of-wedlock pregnancies and establish annual numerical goals for preventing and reducing the incidence of these pregnancies; and (4) encourage the formation and maintenance of two-parent families.

PURPOSE: HHS is encouraging states to consider new, more effective ways to meet the goals of TANF, particularly helping parents successfully prepare for, find, and retain employment. Therefore, HHS is issuing this information memorandum to notify states of the Secretary's willingness to exercise her waiver authority under section 1115 of the Social Security Act to allow states to test alternative and innovative strategies, policies, and procedures that are designed to improve employment outcomes for needy families.

States led the way on welfare reform in the 1990s — testing new approaches and learning what worked and what did not. The Secretary is interested in using her authority to approve waiver demonstrations to challenge states to engage in a new round of innovation that seeks to find more effective mechanisms for helping families succeed in employment. In providing for these demonstrations, HHS will hold states accountable by requiring both a federally-approved evaluation and interim performance targets that ensure an immediate focus on measurable outcomes. States must develop evaluation plans that are sufficient to evaluate the effect of the proposed approach in furthering a TANF purpose as well as interim targets the state commits to achieve. States that fail to meet interim outcome targets will be required to develop an improvement plan and can face termination of the waiver project.

The demonstration authority provided by section 1115 and sound evaluation of approved projects will provide valuable knowledge that will help lead to improvements in achieving the purposes of the TANF program.

INFORMATION: Scope of Authority

Section 1115 authorizes waivers concerning section 402. Accordingly, other provisions of the TANF statute are not waivable. For example, the purposes of TANF are not waivable, because they are contained in section 401. The prohibitions on assistance are not waivable, because they are contained in section 408.

While the TANF work participation requirements are contained in section 407, section 402(a)(1)(A)(iii) requires that the state plan "[e]nsure that parents and caretakers receiving assistance under the program engage in work activities in accordance with section 407." Thus, HHS has authority to waive compliance with this 402 requirement and authorize a state to test approaches and methods other than those set forth in section 407, including definitions of work activities and engagement, specified limitations, verification procedures, and the calculation of participation rates. As described below, however, HHS will only consider approving waivers relating to the work participation requirements that make changes intended to lead to more effective means of meeting the work goals of TANF.

Moreover, HHS is committed to ensuring that any demonstration projects approved under this authority will be focused on improving employment outcomes and contributing to the evidence base for effective programs; therefore, terms and conditions will require a federally-approved evaluation plan designed to build our knowledge base. TANF funds may be used to fund an approved evaluation and state funds spent on an approved evaluation may be considered state maintenance-of-effort (MOE) expenditures. In addition, terms and conditions will require either interim targets for each performance measure or a strategy for establishing baseline performance on a set of performance measures and a framework for how interim goals will be set after the baseline measures are established. The terms and conditions will establish consequences for failing to meet interim performance targets including, but not limited to, the implementation of an improvement plan and, if the failure to meet performance targets continues, termination of the waivers and demonstration project.

HHS Priorities

In exercising her broad discretion for waivers, the Secretary is interested in approaches that seek to improve employment outcomes. Accordingly:

- Waivers will be granted only for provisions related to section 402.
- The purposes of TANF, the prohibitions contained in section 408 (including the time limits on assistance contained in that section), or any other provision of TANF other than those specified in section 402 will not be waived.
- The Secretary will not approve a waiver for an initiative that appears substantially likely to reduce access to assistance or employment for needy families.
- The Secretary will not use her authority to allow use of TANF funds to provide assistance to individuals or families subject to the TANF prohibitions on assistance.
- The Secretary will not waive section 402(a)(5) relating to requirements to provide equitable access to Indians.

- Waiver demonstration projects may be conducted in limited geographic areas or statewide. The Administration for Children and Families (ACF) is interested in more efficient or effective means to promote employment entry, retention, advancement, or access to jobs that offer opportunities for earnings and advancement that will allow participants to avoid dependence on government benefits. The following are examples of projects that states may want to consider – these are illustrative only:
  - Projects that improve coordination with other components of the workforce investment system, including programs operated under the Workforce Investment Act, or to test an innovative approach to use performance-based contracts and management in order to improve employment outcomes.
  - Projects that demonstrate attainment of superior employment outcomes if a state is held accountable for negotiated employment outcomes in lieu of participation rate requirements.
  - Projects under which a state would count individuals in TANF-subsidized jobs but no longer receiving TANF assistance toward participation rates for a specified period of time in conjunction with an

evaluation of the effectiveness of a subsidized jobs strategy.

- Projects that improve collaboration with the workforce and/or post-secondary education systems to test multi-year career pathways models for TANF recipients that combine learning and work.

- Projects that demonstrate strategies for more effectively serving individuals with disabilities, along with an alternative approach to measuring participation and outcomes for individuals with disabilities.

- Projects that test the impact of a comprehensive universal engagement system in lieu of certain participation rate requirements.

- Projects that test systematically extending the period in which vocational educational training or job search/readiness programs count toward participation rates, either generally or for particular subgroups, such as an extended training period for those pursuing a credential. The purpose of such a waiver would be to determine through evaluation whether a program that allows for longer periods in certain activities improves employment outcomes.

Note that this is not a comprehensive list, and HHS will consider other projects consistent with the statute and the guidance provided in this IM. HHS is especially interested in testing approaches that build on existing evidence on successful strategies for improving employment outcomes.

- Waiver requests must include an evaluation plan. In order to provide the strongest evidence about the effectiveness of the demonstration, the preferred evaluation approach is a random assignment methodology, unless the Secretary determines that an alternative approach is more appropriate in light of the demonstration proposed. All evaluation plans and funds to support them must reflect an adequate level of effort and sound methods to produce credible findings. ACF anticipates actively engaging with states to ensure that evaluation plans are appropriate in light of the nature of the demonstration and that the evaluation findings can reasonably be expected to provide information that will enhance understanding of whether the initiative was successful in furthering HHS priorities. ACF staff members are available to work collaboratively with states to develop further or refine the evaluation plan.
- Waiver requests must include a set of performance measures that states will track to monitor ongoing performance and outcomes

throughout the length of the demonstration project, along with the evaluation. Waiver applications must specify interim targets for each performance measure, including a framework for how often the measures will be reported, or a strategy for establishing baseline performance on a set of performance measures and a framework for how interim goals will be set after the baseline measures are established. Performance measures must be designed to track improvement across the entire set of families targeted as well as appropriate subgroups. In developing the final terms and conditions for an approved waiver, ACF will work with the state to further refine the appropriate performance measures and interim targets as needed. All approved waivers will include a provision that requires timely reporting to HHS on the agreed upon performance measures and progress toward meeting established interim targets. States that fail to meet interim targets will be required to develop improvement plans. Repeated failure to meet performance benchmarks may lead to the termination of the waiver demonstration pilot.

- The request must specify the proposed length of time for the demonstration project. The final terms and conditions will specify the approved length of the project. Absent special circumstances, the length of an approved project will not exceed five years.

- A state will need to develop and submit a budget that includes the costs of program evaluation. TANF and state MOE funds can be used for the costs of evaluation, including third party contributions counting toward meeting a state's MOE requirement.
- HHS recognizes the importance of public input into the process of developing and implementing a waiver demonstration project. Therefore, the state must provide the public with a meaningful opportunity to provide input into the decision-making process prior to the time a proposal is approved by HHS. Further guidance concerning this requirement will be forthcoming.
- Waivers are subject to HHS and Office of Management and Budget (OMB) approval and terms and conditions may include additional requirements, such as site visits, before implementation.

Terms and conditions will require periodic reporting on how the implementation and operation of the demonstration is progressing, including reporting on the performance measures, in addition to evaluation reports. To support learning and knowledge development, ACF staff may conduct on-site visits to observe demonstration operations and meet with relevant managers and staff.

White Folks Guide to Understanding the Black Community

4. 112TH CONGRESS

2D SESSION

H. R. 6140

To prohibit waivers relating to compliance with the work requirements for

the program of block grants to States for temporary assistance for

needy families, and for other purposes.

IN THE HOUSE OF REPRESENTATIVES

JULY 18, 2012

Mr. CAMP (for himself, Mr. KLINE, and Mr. JORDAN) introduced the following bill; which was referred to the Committee on Ways and Means, and in addition to the Committee on Education and the Workforce, for a period to be subsequently determined by the Speaker, in each case for consideration of such provisions as fall within the jurisdiction of the committee concerned

A BILL

To prohibit waivers relating to compliance with the work

requirements for the program of block grants to States

for temporary assistance for needy families, and for other

purposes.

1 Be it enacted by the Senate and House of Representatives

2 of the United States of America in Congress assembled,

3 SECTION 1. SHORT TITLE.

4 This Act may be cited as the "Preserving Work

5 Requirements for Welfare Programs Act of 2012".

VerDate Mar 15 2010 03:22 Jul 20, 2012 Jkt 019200 PO 00000 Frm 00001 Fmt 6652 Sfmt 6201 E:\BILLS\H6140.IH H6140

jbell on DSK7SPTVN1PROD with BILLS2

•HR 6140 IH

1 SEC. 2. FINDINGS.

2 Congress finds the following:

3 (1) The bipartisan 1996 welfare reforms succeeded

4 as a result of their pro-work focus, as demonstrated

5 by the following:

6 (A) Research has shown that 65 percent of

7 families receiving welfare through the former

8 Aid to Families with Dependent Children

9 (AFDC) program, which lacked effective work

10 requirements and was replaced by the 1996

11 welfare reform law (P.L. 104–193), remained

12 on welfare for 8 or more years, and the average

13 lifetime receipt of welfare for families then

14 receiving benefits was 13 years.

15 (B) The 1996 welfare reform law replaced

16 the failed AFDC program with the Temporary

17 Assistance for Needy Families (TANF) block

18 grant program, which made promoting work a

19 central focus of each State's efforts to assist

20 low-income parents in achieving self-sufficiency.

21 (C) The 1996 welfare reforms resulted

22 in—

23 (i) significant increases in the employment

24 and earnings of single mothers;

VerDate Mar 15 2010 03:22 Jul 20, 2012 Jkt 019200 PO 00000 Frm 00002 Fmt 6652 Sfmt 6201 E:\BILLS\H6140.IH H6140

jbell on DSK7SPTVN1PROD with BILLS3

•HR 6140 IH

1 (ii) record declines in welfare dependency

2 as TANF rolls fell by more than 57

3 percent; and

4 (iii) significant reductions in child

5 poverty in female-headed households, which

6 even after the impact of a deep recession

7 are still below pre-reform levels.

8 (2) The authors of the 1996 welfare reforms

9 did not intend for States to be able to "waive" this

10 pro-work focus, as indicated by the following:

11 (A) In the 1996 welfare reform law, Congress

12 created specific new work requirements

13 for welfare recipients.

14 (B) In the 1996 welfare reform law, Congress

15 allowed States some limited waiver authority

16 over only TANF State plan requirements

17 which require the State to describe how

18 they intend to carry out various TANF program

19 requirements.

20 (C) In section 1115 of the Social Security

21 Act, Congress specifically did not authorize

22 States to seek, or the Secretary of Health and

23 Human Services to award, waivers involving

24 TANF work requirements. In section 415 of

25 the Social Security Act, Congress specified that

VerDate Mar 15 2010 03:22 Jul 20, 2012 Jkt 019200 PO 00000 Frm 00003 Fmt 6652 Sfmt 6201 E:\BILLS\H6140.IH H6140

jbell on DSK7SPTVN1PROD with BILLS4

•HR 6140 IH

1 any waivers subsequently approved could not

2 waive features of those work requirements.

3 (D) In a Congressional summary published

4 immediately after enactment of the 1996 reforms,

5 the authors of the 1996 welfare reform

6 law summarized its intended treatment of waivers

7 as follows: "Waivers granted after the date

8 of enactment may not override provisions of the

9 TANF law that concern mandatory work

10 requirements.".

11 (3) The recent Department of Health and

12 Human Services Information Memorandum dated

13 July 12, 2012, suggesting States may waive this

14 pro-work focus should be immediately withdrawn by

15 the Obama Administration, or repealed through this

16 legislation, for the following reasons:

17 (A) In the 16 years since enactment of the

18 1996 welfare reforms, no previous Secretary of

19 Health and Human Services has ever asserted

20 that he or she has authority to grant waivers

21 involving TANF work requirements.

22 (B) Despite this fact, and without any

23 prior Obama Administration legislative proposal

24 or consultation with Congress, on July 12,

25 2012, the Department of Health and Human

VerDate Mar 15 2010 03:40 Jul 20, 2012 Jkt 019200 PO 00000 Frm 00004 Fmt 6652 Sfmt 6201 E:\BILLS\H6140.IH H6140

jbell on DSK7SPTVN1PROD with BILLS5

•HR 6140 IH

1 Services unilaterally determined that the Secretary

2 could permit States to waive statutory

3 work requirements for welfare recipients.

4 (C) The Secretary should repeal the July

5 12, 2012 Information Memorandum and make

6 it clear once again that States do not have

7 authority to seek, and the Secretary does not have

8 the authority to grant, waivers of work requirements

9 under the TANF program, consistent

10 with longstanding interpretation of TANF law.

11 SEC. 3. PROHIBITION ON TANF WAIVERS RELATING TO

12 COMPLIANCE WITH THE TANF WORK RE-

13 QUIREMENTS.

14 (a) IN GENERAL.—Notwithstanding any other provision

15 of law, the Secretary of Health and Human Services

16 may not do the following:

17 (1) Finalize, implement, enforce, or otherwise

18 take any action to give effect to the Information

19 Memorandum dated July 12, 2012 (Transmittal No.

20 TANF–ACF–IM–2012–03), or to any administrative

21 action relating to the same subject matter set forth

22 in the Information Memorandum or that reflects the

23 same or similar policies as those set forth in the

24 In formation Memorandum.

VerDate Mar 15 2010 03:22 Jul 20, 2012 Jkt 019200 PO
00000 Frm 00005 Fmt 6652 Sfmt 6201
E:\BILLS\H6140.IH H6140

jbell on DSK7SPTVN1PROD with BILLS6

•HR 6140 IH

1 (2) Authorize, approve, renew, modify, or

2 extend any experimental, pilot, or demonstration

3 project under section 1115 of the Social Security

4 Act (42 U.S.C. 1315) that waives compliance with

5 a requirement of section 407 of such Act (42 U.S.C.

6 607) through a waiver of section 402 of such Act

7 (42 U.S.C. 602) or that provides authority for an

8 expenditure which would not otherwise be an

9 allow able use of funds under a State program funded

10 under part A of title IV of such Act (42 U.S.C. 601

11 et seq.) with respect to compliance with the work

12 requirements in section 407 of such Act to

13 be regarded as an allowable use of funds under that

14 program for any period.

15 (b) RESCISSION OF WAIVERS.—Any waiver relating

16 to the subject matter set forth in the Information

17 Memorandum or described in subsection (a)(2) that is granted

18 before the date of the enactment of this Act is hereby rescinded and shall be null and void.

5. Flat Tax

From Wikipedia, the free encyclopedia

For the term related to tax incidence regarding flat progressivity,

A **flat tax** (short for **flat tax rate**) is a tax system with a constant marginal tax rate. Typically the term *flat tax* is applied in the context of an individual or corporate income that will be taxed at one marginal rate. Flat taxes in application often allow certain deductions and thus are a special case of a proportional tax.

Flat tax proposals differ in how they define what is subject to tax.

"True" flat rate income tax

A *true* flat rate tax is a system of taxation where one tax rate is applied to all income with no deductions or exemptions.

Marginal flat tax

When deductions are allowed a 'flat tax' is a progressive tax with the special characteristic that above the maximum deduction, the rate on all further income is constant. Thus it is said to be marginally flat above that point. The conceptual difference between a true flat tax and a marginally flat tax, can be unified by recognizing that the latter simply excludes certain kinds of funds from being defined as income. Then they are both flat on "taxable" income.

There are many proposed marginal flat taxes systems. Specific flat tax systems enumerated at the bottom of this article primarily intermix aspects of three high level approaches:

Flat tax with limited deductions

Modified flat taxes have been proposed which would allow deductions for a very few items, while still eliminating the vast majority of existing deductions. Charitable deductions and home mortgage interest are the most discussed exceptions, as these are popular with voters and often used. Another common theme is a single, large, fixed deduction; the concept here is that this blanket deduction rolls up a myriad of ubiquitous, fixed, living costs and has the simplifying side-effect that many (low income) people will not even have to file tax returns.

Hall–Rabushka flat tax

Designed by economists at the Hoover Institution, Hall–Rabushka is flat tax on consumption. Principally, Hall–Rabushka accomplishes a consumption tax effect by taxing income and then excluding investment. Robert Hall and Alvin Rabushka have consulted extensively in designing the flat tax systems in Eastern Europe.

Negative income tax

The negative income tax (NIT), which Milton Friedman proposed in his 1962 book *Capitalism and Freedom*, is a type of flat tax. The basic idea is the same as a flat tax with personal deductions, except that when deductions exceed income, the taxable income is allowed to become negative rather than being set to zero. The flat tax rate is then applied to the resulting "negative income," resulting in a "negative income tax" the government owes the household, unlike the usual "positive" income tax, which the household owes the government.

For example, let the flat rate be 20%, and let the deductions be $20,000 per adult and $7,000 per dependent. Under such a system, a family of four making $54,000 a year would owe no tax. A family of four making $74,000 a year would owe tax amounting to $0.20 \times (74,000 - 54,000) = \$4,000$, as under a flat tax with deductions. But families of four earning less than $54,000 per year would owe a "negative" amount of tax (that is, it would receive money from the government). For example, if it earned $34,000 a year, it would receive a check for $4,000. The NIT is intended to replace not just the USA's income tax, but also many benefits low income American households receive, such as food stamps and Medicaid. The NIT is designed to avoid the welfare trap—effective high marginal tax rates arising from the rules reducing benefits as market income rises. An objection to the NIT is that it is welfare without a work requirement. Those who would owe negative tax would be receiving a form of welfare without having to make an effort to obtain employment. Another objection is that the NIT subsidizes industries employing low cost labor, but this objection can also be made against current systems of benefits for the working poor.

Capped flat tax

A **capped** flat tax is one in which income is taxed at a flat rate until a specified cap is reached. For example, in 2010, the United States payroll tax assessed a flat rate of 15.3% on all income under $106,800 and only 1.45% above that level. Thus, someone earning $100,000 paid $15,300 (a rate of 15.3%) while someone earning $1,000,000 paid $28,350 (a rate of 2.8%). This cap has the effect of turning a nominally flat tax into a regressive tax.

Defining when income occurs

Since a central philosophy of the flat tax is to minimize the compartmentalization of incomes into myriad special or sheltered cases, a vexing problem is deciding when income occurs. This is demonstrated by the taxation of interest income and stock dividends. The shareholders own the company and so the company's profits belong to them. If a company is taxed on its profits, then the funds paid out as dividends have already been taxed. It's a debatable question if they should subsequently be treated as income to the shareholders and thus subject to further tax. A similar issue arises in deciding if interest paid on loans should be deductible from the taxable income since that interest is in-turn taxed as income to the loan provider. There is no universally agreed answer to what is fair. For example, in the United States, dividends are not deductible but mortgage interest is deductible *Thus a Flat Tax proposal is not fully defined until it differentiates* new *untaxed income from a pass-through of already taxed income.*

Policy administration

Taxes, in addition to providing revenue, can be potent instruments of policy. For example, it is common for governments to encourage social policy such as home insulation or low income housing with tax credits rather than constituting a ministry to implement these policies. In a flat tax system with limited deductions such policy administration mechanisms are curtailed. In addition to social policy, flat taxes can remove tools for adjusting economic policy as well. For example, in the US short term gains are taxed at a higher rate than long term gains as means to promote long term investment horizons and damp speculative fluctuation. *Thus claims that flat taxes are cheaper/simpler to administer than others are incomplete until they factor in costs for alternative policy administration.*

White Folks Guide to Understanding the Black Community

Avoiding deductions

In general, the question of how to eliminate deductions is fundamental to the flat tax design: deductions dramatically affect the effective "flatness" in the tax rate. Perhaps the single biggest necessary deduction is for business expenses. If businesses were not allowed to deduct expenses then businesses with a profit margin below the flat tax rate could never earn any money since the tax on revenues would always exceed the earnings. For example, grocery stores typically earn pennies on every dollar of revenue; they could not pay a tax rate of 25% on revenues unless their markup exceeded 25%.

Thus corporations must be able to deduct operating expenses even if individual citizens cannot. A practical difficulty now arises as to identifying what is an expense for a business. For example, if a peanut butter maker purchases a jar manufacturer, is that an expense (since they have to purchase jars somehow) or a sheltering of their income through investment? Flat tax systems can differ greatly in how they accommodate such gray areas. For example, the "9-9-9" flat tax proposal would allow businesses to deduct purchases but not labor costs. (And thus effectively tax labor intensive industrial revenue at a higher rate.) How deductions are implemented will dramatically change the effective total tax, and thus flatness, of the tax *Thus a Flat Tax proposal is not fully defined until it differentiates deductible and non-deductible expenses.*

Equity of distribution

Tax distribution across varying income levels is a hotly debated aspect of flat taxes. The question of fairness is centered on what tax deductions are abolished when a flat tax is introduced, and who is most affected by the abolition of those deductions. The controversy over the equity of distribution can be divided into fundamental implementation and philosophical issues. Identification of philosophical issues is important for governments moving towards a flat tax, as the ideals of financial fairness are the starting point for comparison.

Diminishing Marginal Utility

One of the concerns with many flat tax systems is that they are not true flat taxes, which in turn makes the debate over the equitability of the tax difficult. If a system has a large per-citizen deductible (such as the "Armey" scheme below), then it is a progressive tax – one where the tax rate on total income increases as income increases. As a result, sometimes the term Flat Tax is actually a shorthand for the more proper marginally flat tax.

Proponents of the flat tax claim a single marginal rate is more fair than stepped marginal tax rates (a.k.a. "progressive"), since everybody pays the same proportion of taxable income. Critics of the flat tax, on the other hand, claim that the marginal value of income declines with the amount of income (the last $100 of income of a family living near poverty being considerably more valuable than the last $100 of income of a millionaire), and thus assert that taxing that last $100 of income the same amount despite vast differences in the marginal value of money is unfair. Flat tax proponents contest the concept of *the diminishing marginal utility of money* and that a marginal dollar should be taxed differently.

Effects on government spending

Proponents of the flat tax system point out that there is a strong likelihood that another positive effect would be to discourage increased spending by government. The reason for this would be that any tax increase would affect all taxpayers. In the current tax system, government officials are able to win the approval of the public by raising taxes on certain groups to pay for new spending. If everyone's taxes had to go up with any new spending, every new government program would have to be carefully scrutinized. In the long run, the hope would be that government would become more efficient.

Administration and enforcement

One type of flat tax taxes all income once at its source. Hall and Rabushka (1995) includes a proposed amendment to the US Revenue Code implementing the variant of the flat tax they advocate. This amendment, only a few pages long, would replace hundreds of pages of statutory language (although it is important to note that much statutory language in taxation statutes is *not* directed at specifying graduated tax rates). As it now stands, the USA Revenue Code is over 9 million words long[j] and contains many loopholes, deductions, and exemptions which, advocates of flat taxes claim, render the collection of taxes and the enforcement of tax law complicated and inefficient. It is further argued that current tax law retards economic growth by distorting economic incentives, and by allowing, even encouraging, tax avoidance. With a flat tax, there are fewer incentives than in the current system to create tax shelters and to engage in other forms of tax avoidance. Flat tax critics contend that a flat tax system could be created with many loopholes, or a progressive tax system without loopholes, and that a progressive tax system could be as simple, or simpler, than a flat tax system. A simple progressive tax would also discourage tax avoidance.

Under a pure flat tax without deductions, companies could simply, every period, make a single payment to the government covering the flat tax liabilities of their employees and the taxes owed on their business income. For example, suppose that in a given year, ACME earns a profit of 3 million, pays 2 million in salaries, and spends an added 1 million on other expenses the IRS deems to be taxable income, such as stock options, bonuses, and certain executive privileges. Given a flat rate of 15%, ACME would then owe the IRS (3M + 2M + 1M) × 0.15 =

900,000. This payment would, in one fell swoop, settle the tax liabilities of ACME's employees as well as taxes it owed by being a firm. Most employees throughout the economy would never need to interact with the IRS, as all tax owed on wages, interest, dividends, royalties, etc. would be withheld at the source. The main exceptions would be employees with incomes from personal ventures. The *Economist* claims that such a system would reduce the number of entities required to file returns from about 130 million individuals, households, and businesses, as at present, to a mere 8 million businesses and self-employed.

However this simplicity relies on there being no deductions of any kind allowed (or at least no variability in the deductions of different people). Furthermore if income of differing types are segregated (e.g. pass-thru, long term cap gains, regular income,) then complications ensue. For example, if realized capital gains were subject to the flat tax, the law would require brokers and mutual funds to calculate the realized capital gain on all sales and redemption. If there were a gain, 15% of the gain would be withheld and sent to the IRS. If there were a loss, the amount would be reported to the IRS, which would offset gains with losses and settle up with taxpayers at the end of the period. Lacking deductions this scheme cannot be used to implement economic and social policy indirectly by tax credits, and thus, as noted above, the simplifications to the government's revenue collection apparatus may be offset by new government ministries required to administer those policies.

Revenues

The Russian Federation is a considered a prime case of the success of a flat tax; the real revenues from its Personal Income Tax rose by 25.2% in the first year after the Federation introduced a flat tax, followed by a 24.6% increase in the second year, and a 15.2% increase in the third year. The Laffer curve predicts such an outcome, attributing the primary reason for the greater revenue to higher levels of economic growth stemming from the introduction of the flat tax.

The Russian example is often used as proof of the validity of this analysis, despite an International Monetary Fund study in 2006 which found that there was no sign "of Laffer-type behavioral responses generating revenue increases from the tax cut elements of these reforms" in Russia or in other countries.

Overall structure

Taxes other than the income tax (for example, taxes on sales and payrolls) tend to be regressive. Hence, making the income tax flat could result in a regressive overall tax structure. Under such a structure, those with lower incomes tend to pay a *higher* proportion of their income in total taxes than the affluent do. The fraction of household income that is a return to capital (dividends, interest, royalties, profits of unincorporated businesses) is positively correlated with total household income Hence a flat tax limited to wages would seem to leave the wealthy better off. Modifying the tax base can change the effects. A flat tax could be targeted at income (rather than wages), which could place the tax burden equally on all earners, including those who earn income primarily from returns on investment. Tax systems could utilize a flat sales tax to target all consumption, which can be modified with rebates or exemptions to remove regressive effects (such as the proposed FairTax in the U.S.).

Border adjustable

A flat tax system and income taxes overall are not inherently border-adjustable; meaning the tax component embedded into products via taxes imposed on companies (including corporate taxesand payroll taxes) are not removed when exported to a foreign country *(see Effect of taxes and subsidies on price)*. Taxation systems such as a sales tax or value added tax can remove the tax component when goods are exported and apply the tax component on imports. The domestic products could be at a disadvantage to foreign products (at home and abroad) that are border-adjustable, which would impact the global competitiveness of a country. However, it's possible that a flat tax system could be combined with tariffs and credits to act as border adjustments (the proposed *Border Tax Equity Act* in the U.S. attempts this). Implementing an income tax with a border

adjustment tax credit is a violation of the World Trade
Organization agreement. Tax exemptions (allowances) on low
income wages, a component of most income tax systems could
mitigate this issue for high labour content industries like textiles
that compete Globally.

Tax simplification

Flat tax has been proposed as a means of simplifying the tax
code from the current progressive or graduated marginal tax
rates. Yet of the 72,000+ pages in the US tax code as of 2009,
less than a quarter of one of those pages is needed to list the
progressive marginal tax rates. Calculating the progressive tax
after determining the net taxable income may be the simplest
activity one performs in manually calculating one's income tax
liability. Extreme simplification could be achieved by merely
eliminating all tax deductions, exclusions, subsidies, rebates etc.
and retaining the six tier progressive marginal tax structure.

Flat tax proposals have made something of a "comeback" in
recent years. In the United States, former House Majority
Leader Dick Armey and FreedomWorks have sought support for
the flat tax (Taxpayer Choice Act). In other countries, flat tax
systems have also been proposed, largely as a result of flat tax
systems being introduced in several countries of the
former Eastern Bloc, where it is generally thought to have been

successful, although this assessment has been disputed (see below).

The countries that have recently reintroduced flat taxes have done so largely in the hope of boosting economic growth. The Baltic countries of Estonia, Latvia and Lithuania have had flat taxes of 24%, 25% and 33% respectively with a tax exempt amount, since the mid-1990s. On 1 January 2001, a 13% flat tax on personal income took effect in Russia. Ukraine followed Russia with a 13% flat tax in 2003, which later increased to 15% in 2007. Slovakia introduced a 19% flat tax on most taxes (that is, on corporate and personal income, for VAT, etc., almost without exceptions) in 2004; Romania introduced a 16% flat tax on personal income and corporate profit on 1 January 2005. Macedonia introduced a 12% flat tax on personal income and corporate profit on 1 January 2007 and promised to cut it to 10% in 2008. Albania has implemented a 10% flat tax from 2008. Bulgaria applies flat tax rate of 10% for corporate profits and personal income tax since 2008.

In the United States, while the Federal income tax is progressive, seven states —
Colorado, Illinois, Indiana, Massachusetts, Michigan, Pennsylvania, and Utah — tax household incomes at a single rate, ranging from 3.07% (Pennsylvania) to 5.3% (Massachusetts).

Pennsylvania even has a *pure* flat tax with no zero-bracket amount.

Paul Kirchhof, who was suggested as the next finance minister of Germany in 2005, proposed introducing a flat tax rate of 25% in Germany as early as 2001, which sparked widespread controversy. Some claim the German tax system is the most complex one in the world.

On 27 September 2005, the Dutch Council of Economic Advisors recommended a flat rate of 40% for income tax in the Netherlands. Some deductions would be allowed, and persons over 65 years of age would be taxed at a lower rate.

In the United States, proposals for a flat tax at the federal level have emerged repeatedly in recent decades during various political debates. Jerry Brown, former and current Democratic Governor of California, made the adoption of a flat tax part of his platform when running for President of the United States in 1992. At the time, rival Democratic candidate Tom Harkin ridiculed the proposal as having originated with the "Flat Earth Society". Four years later, Republican candidate Steve Forbes proposed a similar idea as part of his core platform. Although neither captured his party's nomination, their proposals prompted widespread debate about the current U.S. income tax system.

White Folks Guide to Understanding the Black Community

Flat tax plans that are presently being advanced in the United States also seek to redefine "sources of income"; current progressive taxes count interest, dividends and capital gains as income, for example, while Steve Forbes's variant of the flat tax would apply to wages only.

In 2005 Senator Sam Brownback, a Republican from Kansas, stated he had a plan to implement a flat tax in Washington, D.C.. This version is one flat rate of 15% on all earned income. Unearned income (in particular capital gains) would be exempt. His plan also calls for an exemption of $30,000 per family and $25,000 for singles. Mississippi Republican Senator Trent Lott stated he supports it and would add a $5,000 credit for first time home buyers and exemptions for out of town businesses. DC Delegate Eleanor Holmes Norton's position seems unclear, however DC mayor Anthony Williams has stated he is "open" to the idea.

Flat taxes have also been considered in the United Kingdom by the Conservative Party. In September 2005, George Osborne, then in opposition, said that while he was "fully conscious that we may not be able to introduce a pure flat tax, we may be able to move towards simpler and flatter taxes." However, it was roundly rejected by Gordon Brown, then the Labour Chancellor of the Exchequer, who said that it was "An idea that they say is sweeping the world, well sweeping Estonia, well a wing of the neo-conservatives in Estonia", and criticized it thus: "The millionaire to pay exactly the same tax rate as the young nurse, the home help, the worker on the minimum wage".

Bibliography

Healthcare

http://www.camdenhealth.org/about/about-the-coalition/history/

http://www.newyorker.com/reporting/2011/01/24/110124fa_fact_gawande?currentPage=6

Get out the vote

http://academic.udayton.edu/race/04needs/98newburg.htm

http://rightblack.hubpages.com/hub/Why-Do-Blacks-Vote-Democrat

http://politicalresources.com/Library/GOTV.htm

Education

http://academic.udayton.edu/race/04needs/education05.htm

Tax Reform

http://www.investopedia.com/terms/f/flattax.asp#axzz235R5wyv0

Notes

Chapter 1

1. Stephens, Kuuleme T. Champion of the Ending Slavery, the Civil Rights Movement, and the Black Community." *The Last Civil Right*. 19 Aug. 2012. 20

2. "Is There a Such Thing as a "slave Mentality"?" *Yahoo! Answers*. 21 Aug. 2012.

3. Martin Luther King, Jr. I Have a Dream. New York: Scholastic, 1997.

Chapter 2

4. Hirsch, E. D., Joseph F. Kett, and James S. Trefil. The New Dictionary of Cultural Literacy. Boston: Houghton Mifflin, 2002.
5. The Holy Bible: KJV John 8:7 San Diego, CA: Thunder Bay, 2000.
6. Matthew 7:1 "Bible Gateway." *Bible Gateway*. 21 Aug. 2012.

Chapter 3

7. Tzu, Lao. " Give a Man a Fish and You Feed Him for a Day. Teach a Man How to Fish and You Feed Him for a Lifetime.." *Goodreads*. 21 Aug. 2012.
8. "Frederick Douglass." - *Biography and Works*9. The Holy Bible. KJV Genesis 4:10,

Chapter 4

10. The plantation school, Anthony Gerald. Albanese - Vantage Press - 1976

Chapter 8

Taken from the essay by author Marty Nemko, Closing the Education Gap

Chapter 9

Taken from t he Frederick Douglas Academy for Leadership and Social Change charter school application

Chapter 10

Taken from the National Association of Urban Debate Leagues

The Author:

Pastor Shannon Wright

Pastor Shannon Wright is a former non-profit executive and first Vice President of the Yonkers NAACP who has committed her life to improving public education and creating avenues to enhance the life of today's youth in general. She has always been actively involved in community improvement. In 2004, Wright's family relocated to New Jersey after losing her home to a fire, then a flood immediately afterwards where she quickly became a fixture in community as a pastor, radio personality and ultimately a Youth Guidance Commissioner of her hometown. She also served as the NJ NAACP youth and college advisor along with being a member of the state board of directors.

She believes in the adherence to the Constitution. Shannon uses her voice in the media to encourage individual responsibility, uphold the value of human life, and encourage the break of the cycle of poverty by encouraging choice in education and jobs and opportunities for the youth through tax breaks and public/private partnerships.

Pastor Shannon Wright lives in New Jersey with her husband Michael and their two cats Sam and Dean.